This book belong to

" _____ "

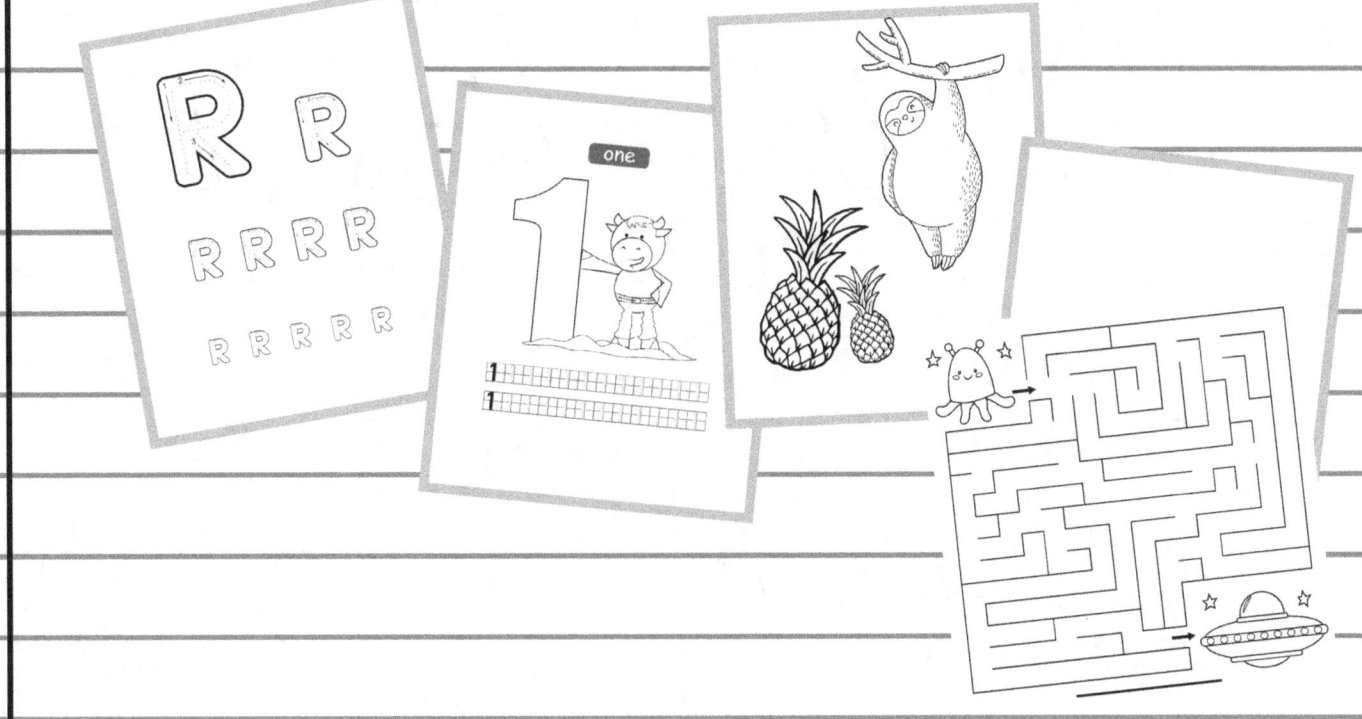

Keep working on it. You're improving

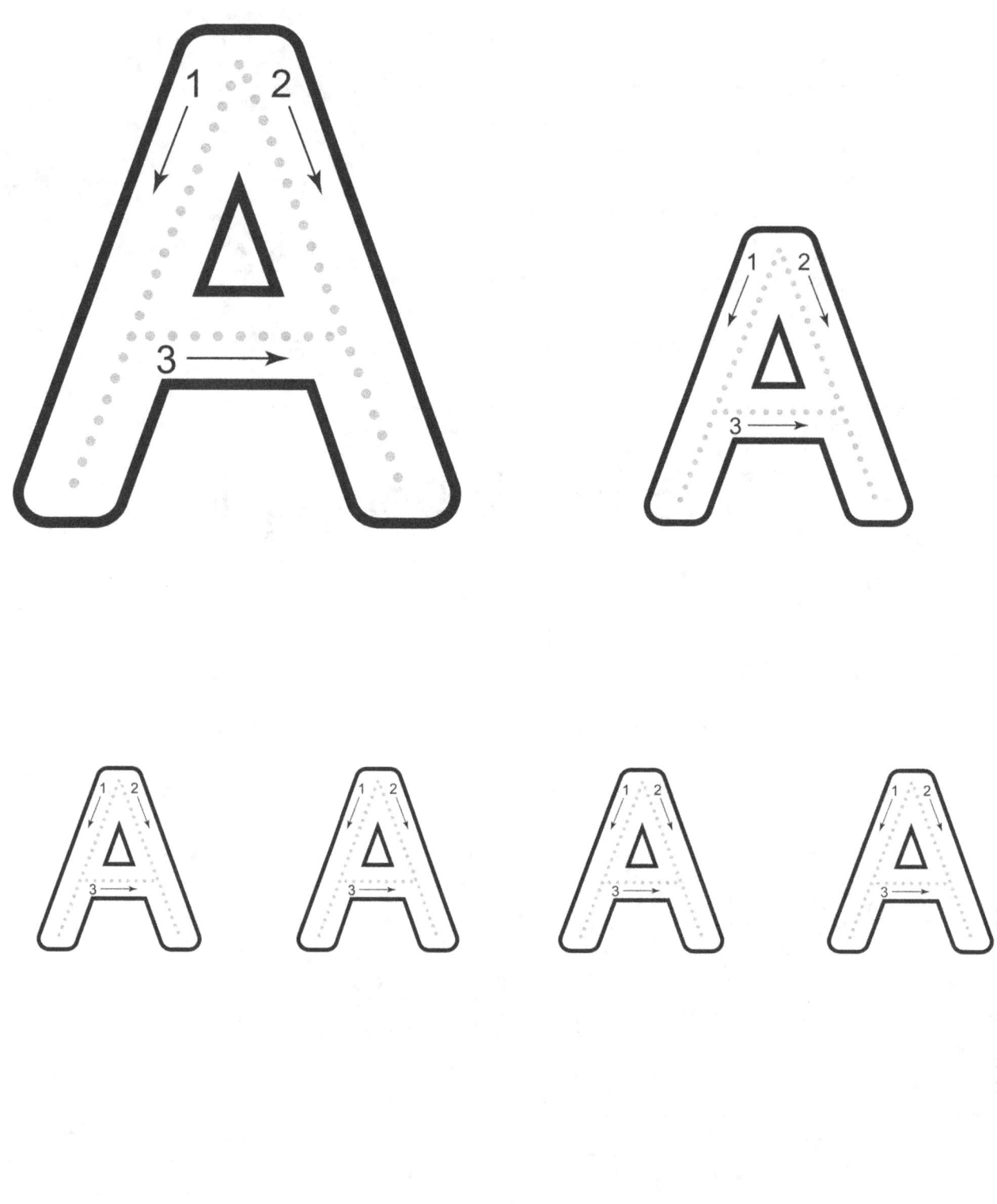

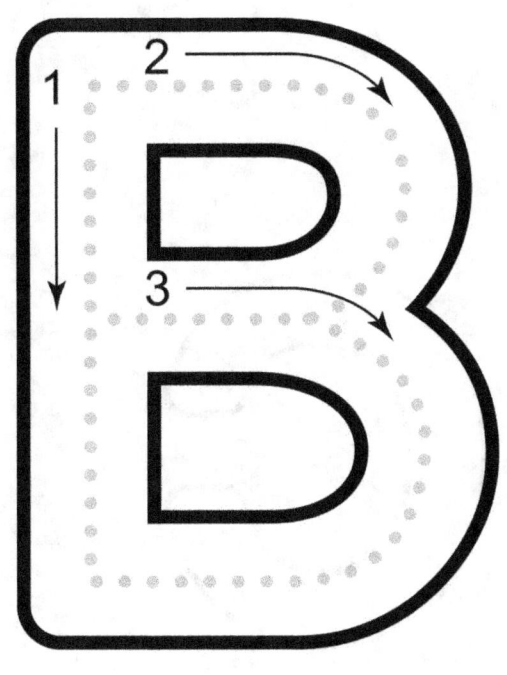 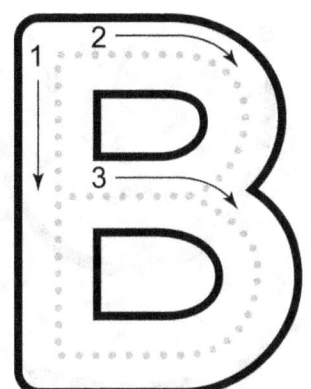

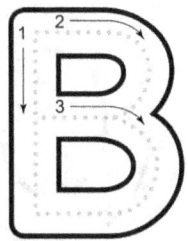 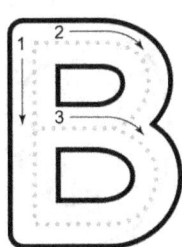 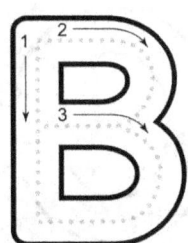 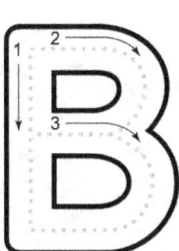

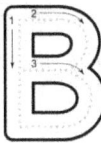 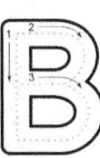 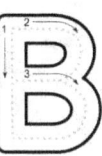 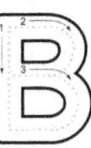 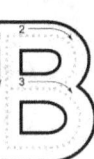 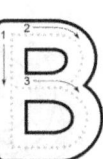

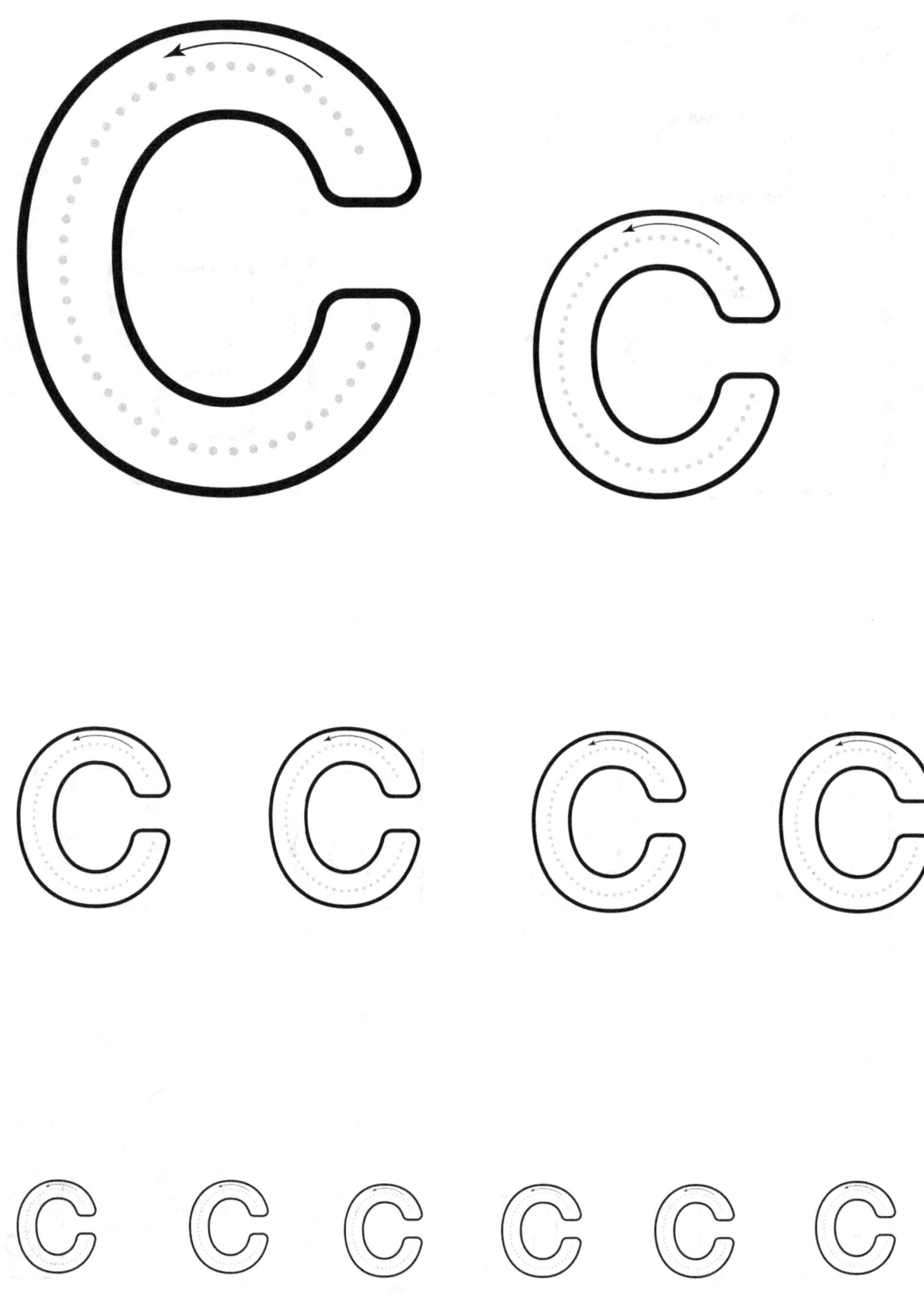

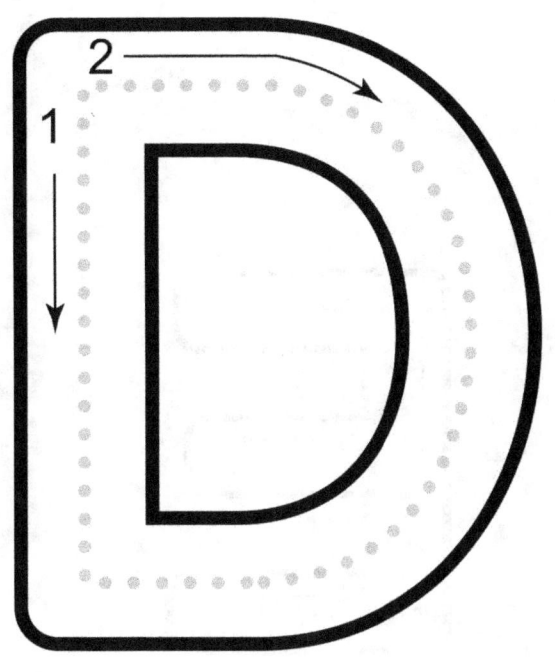 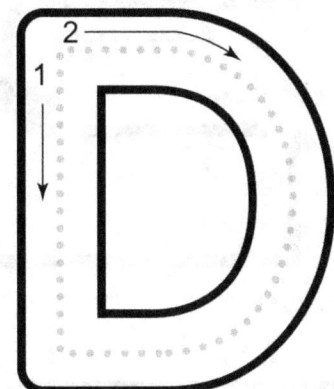

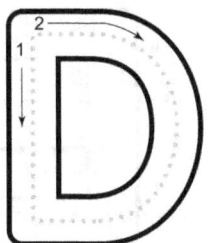 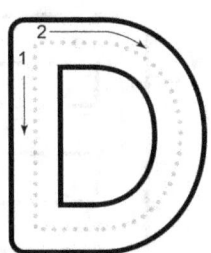 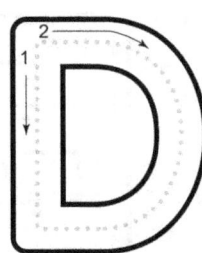 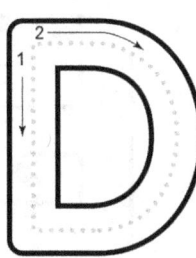

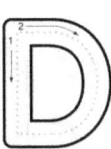 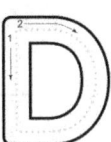 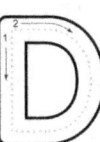 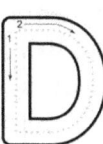 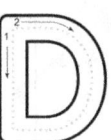

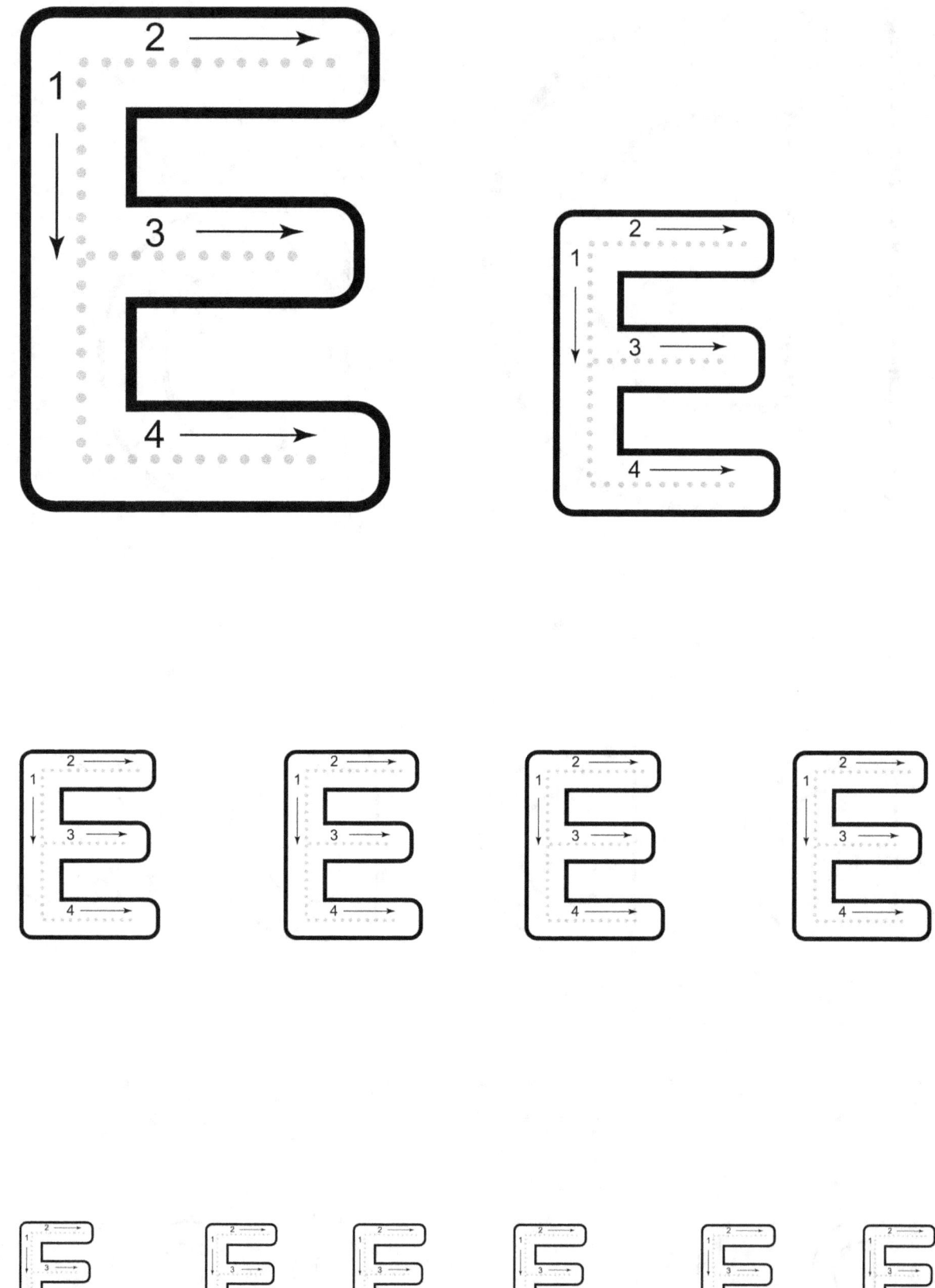

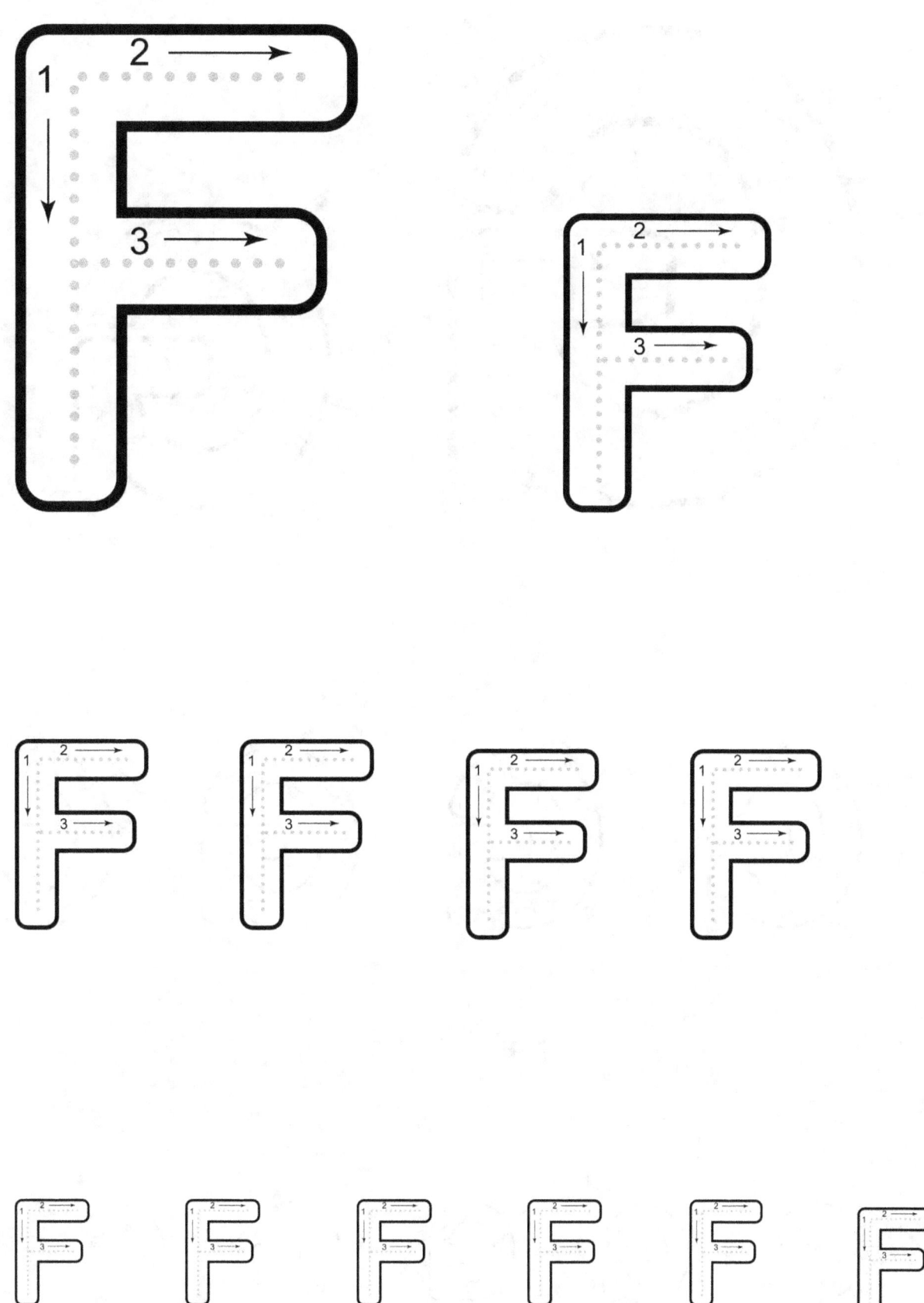

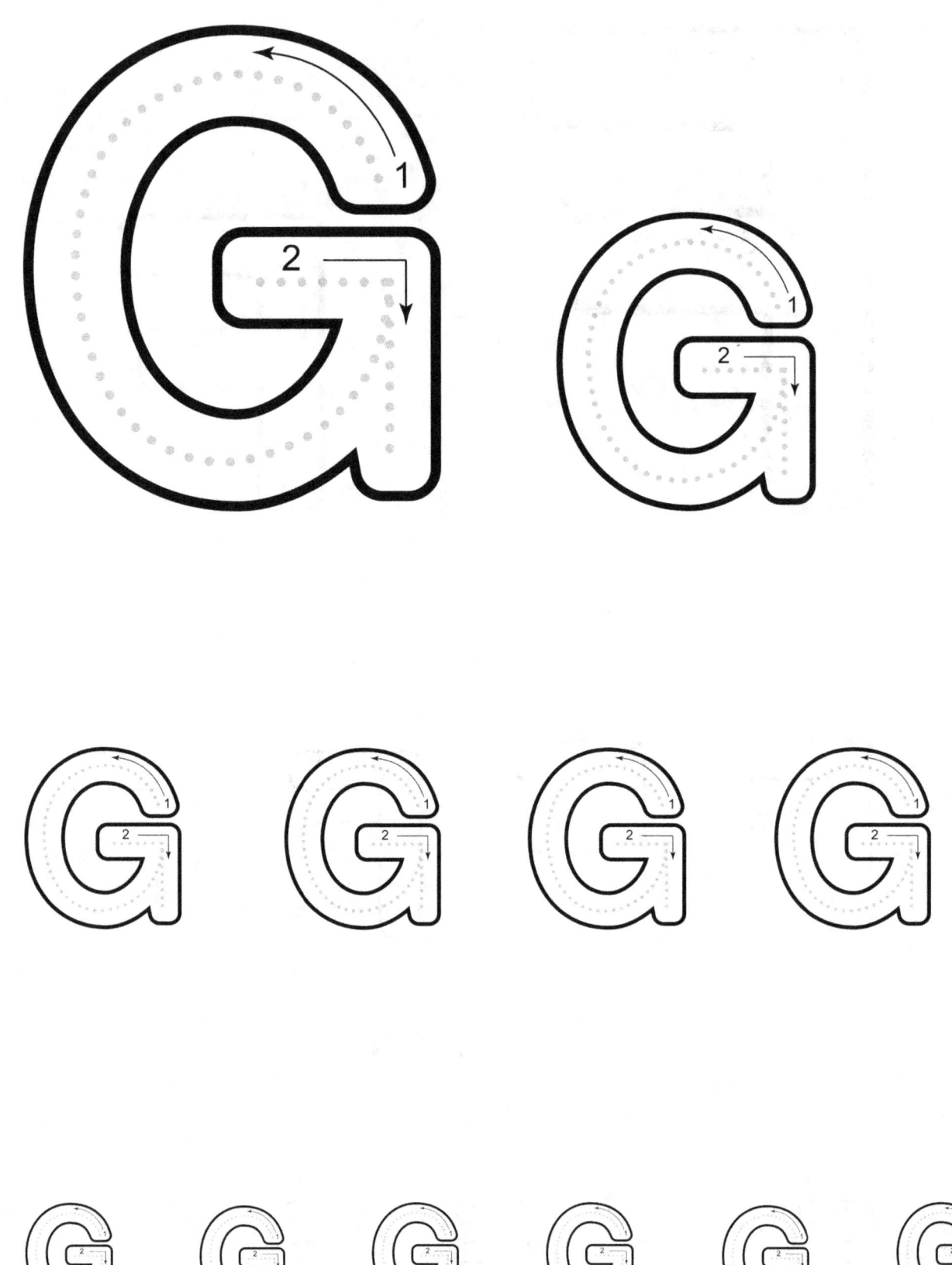

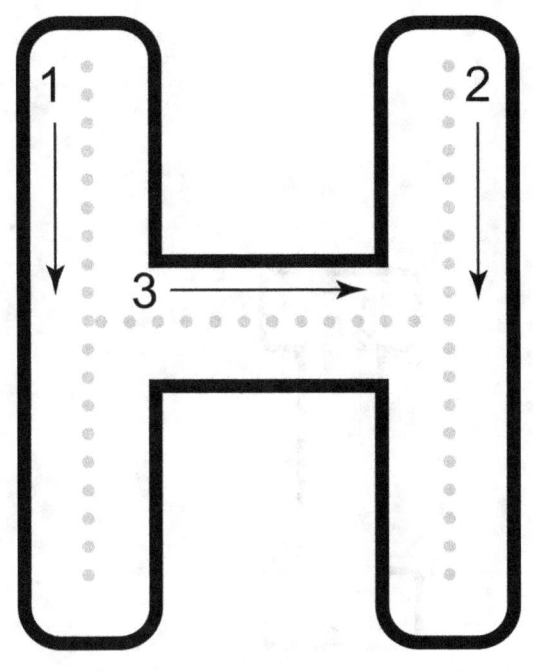
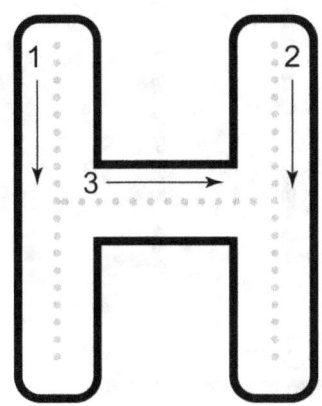
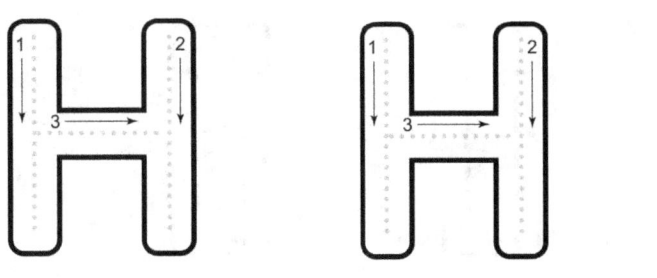
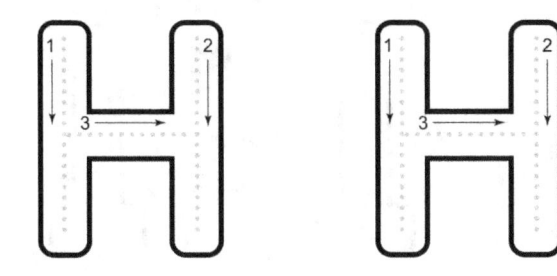

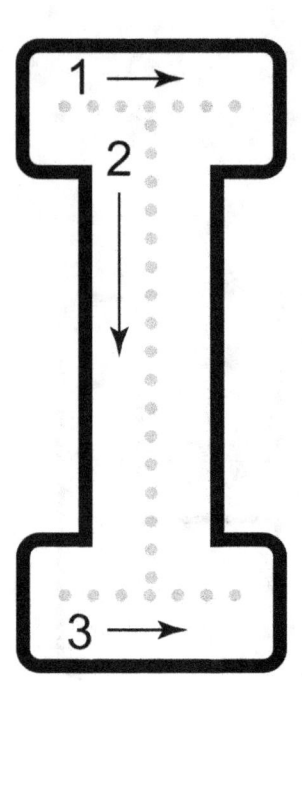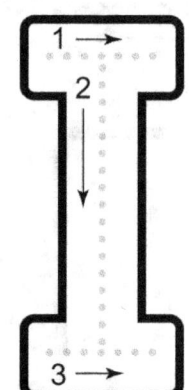

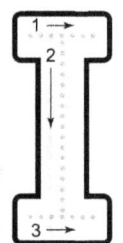 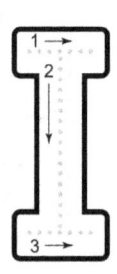 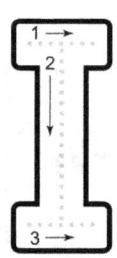 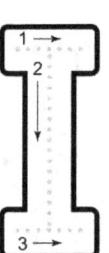

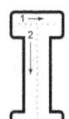 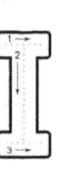 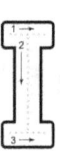 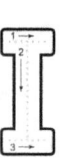 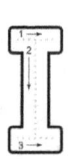 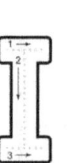 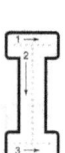

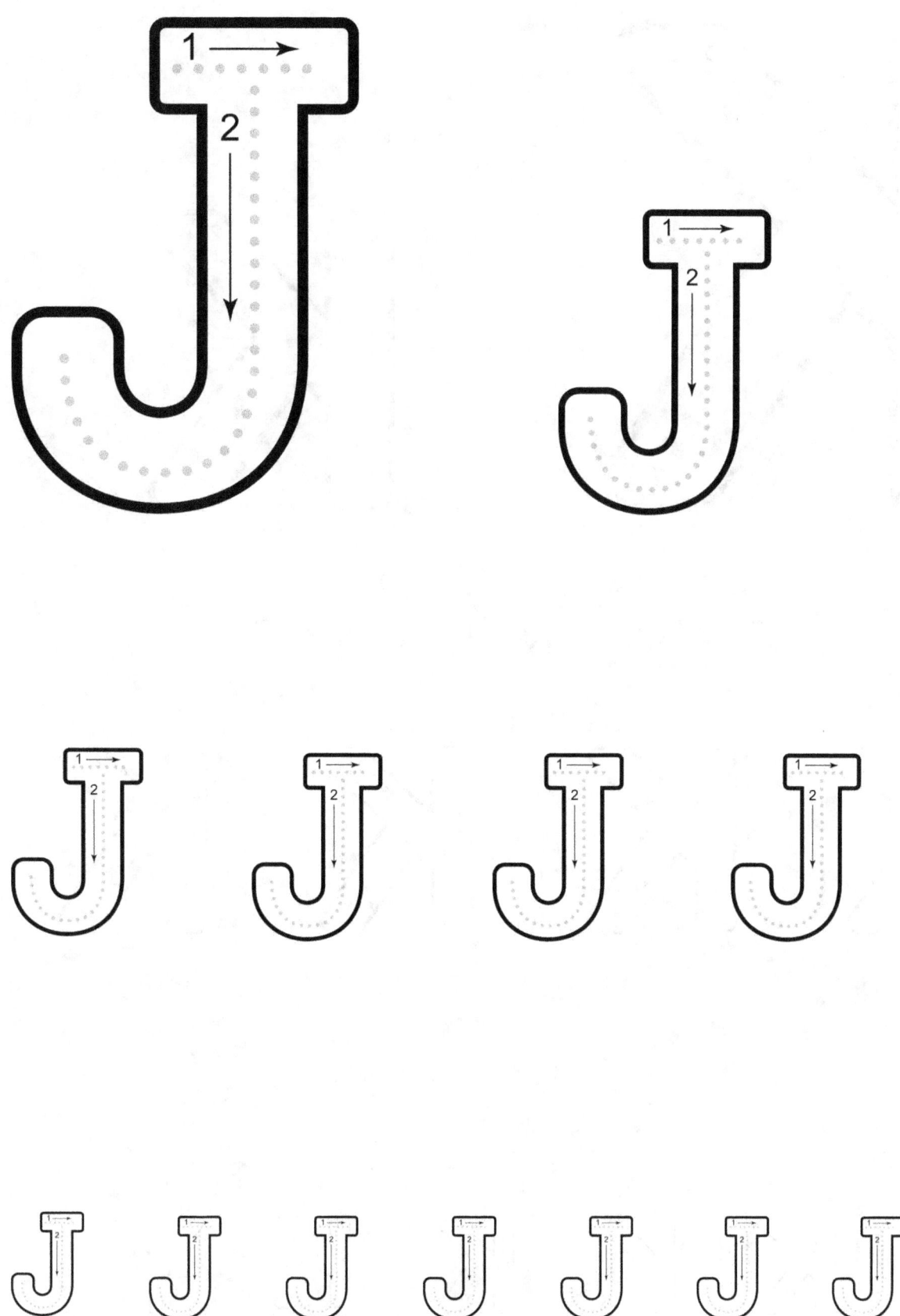

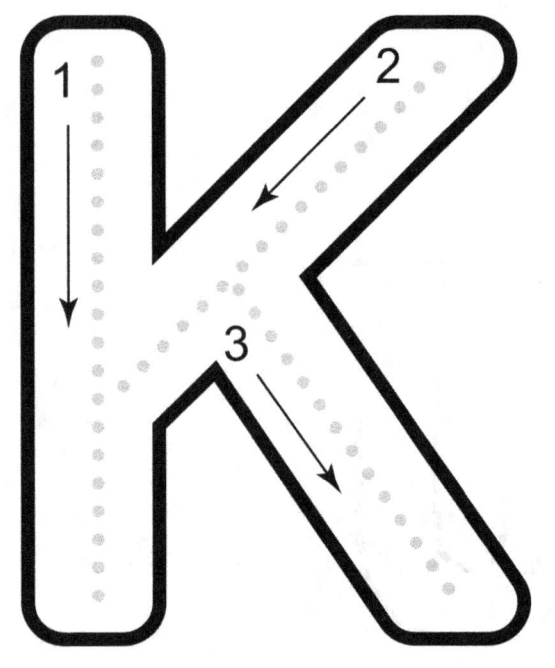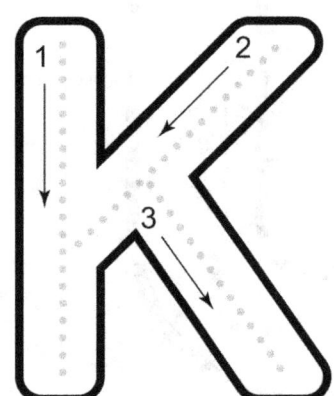

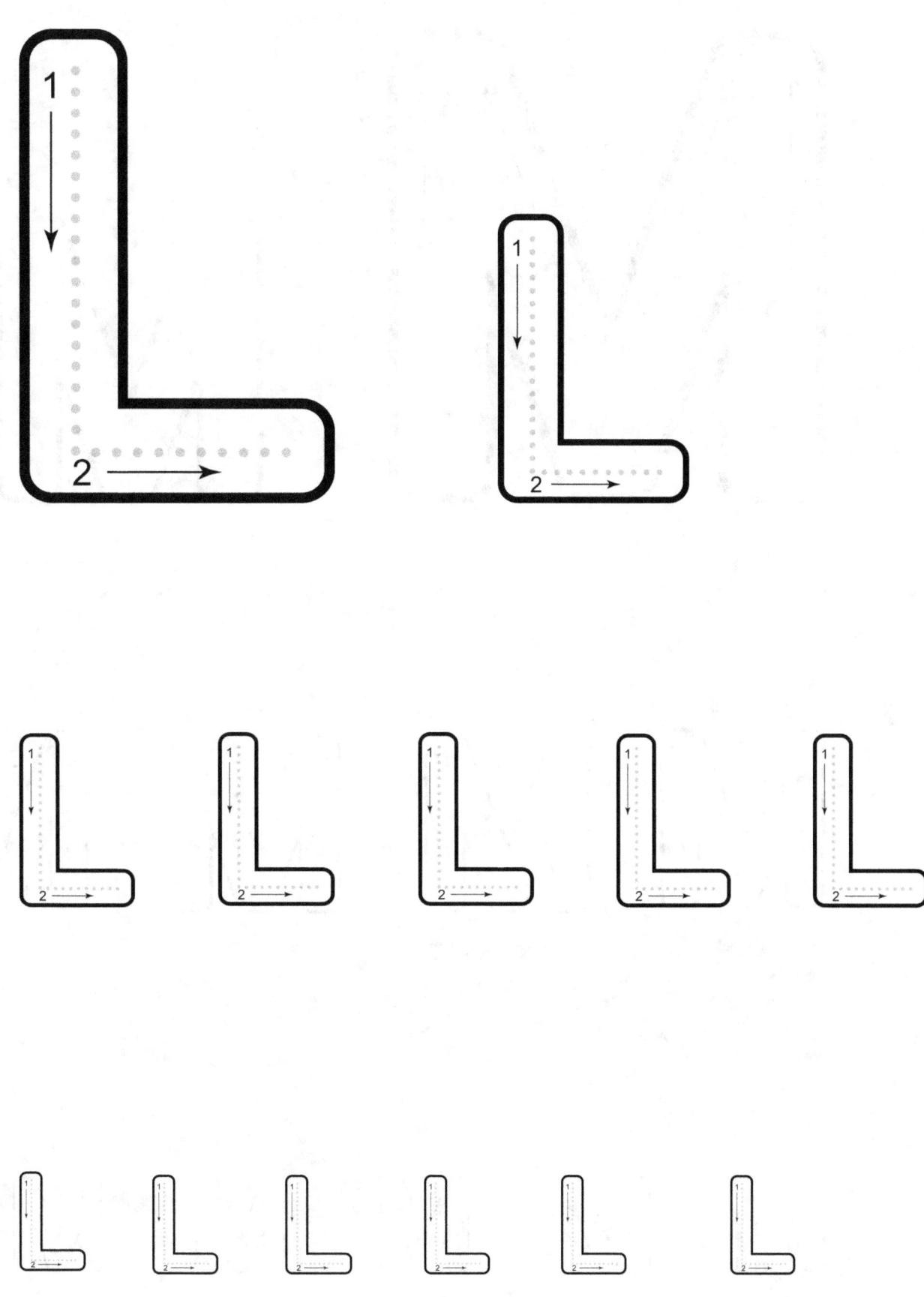

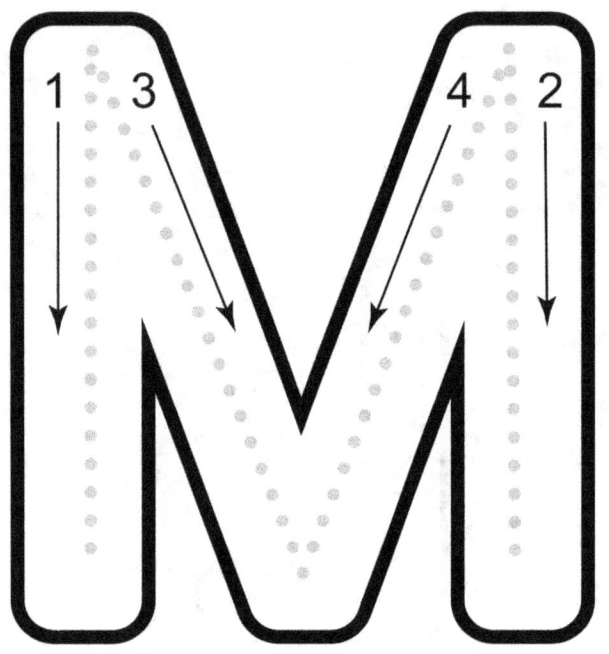
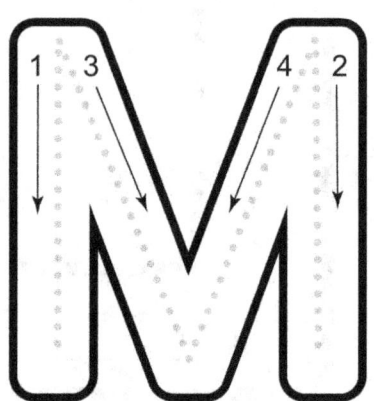

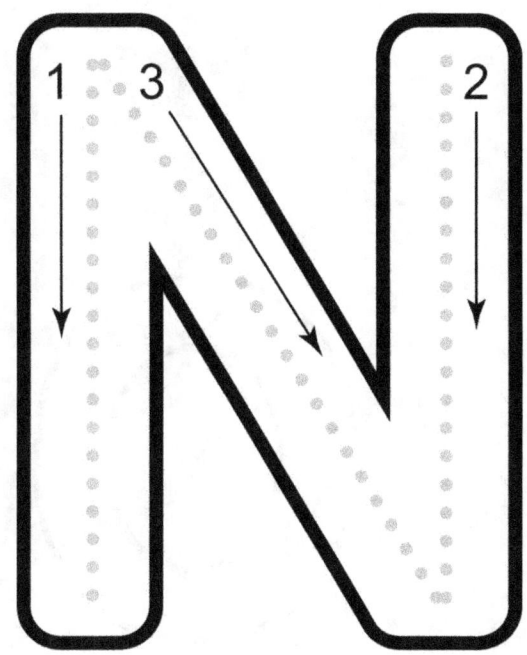 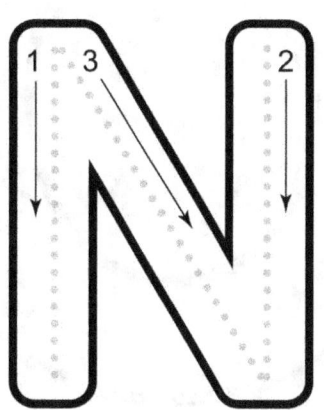

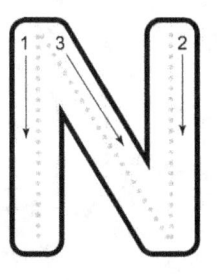 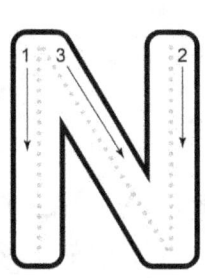 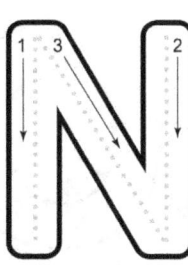 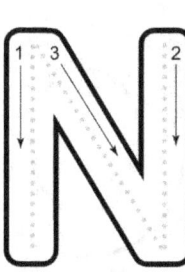

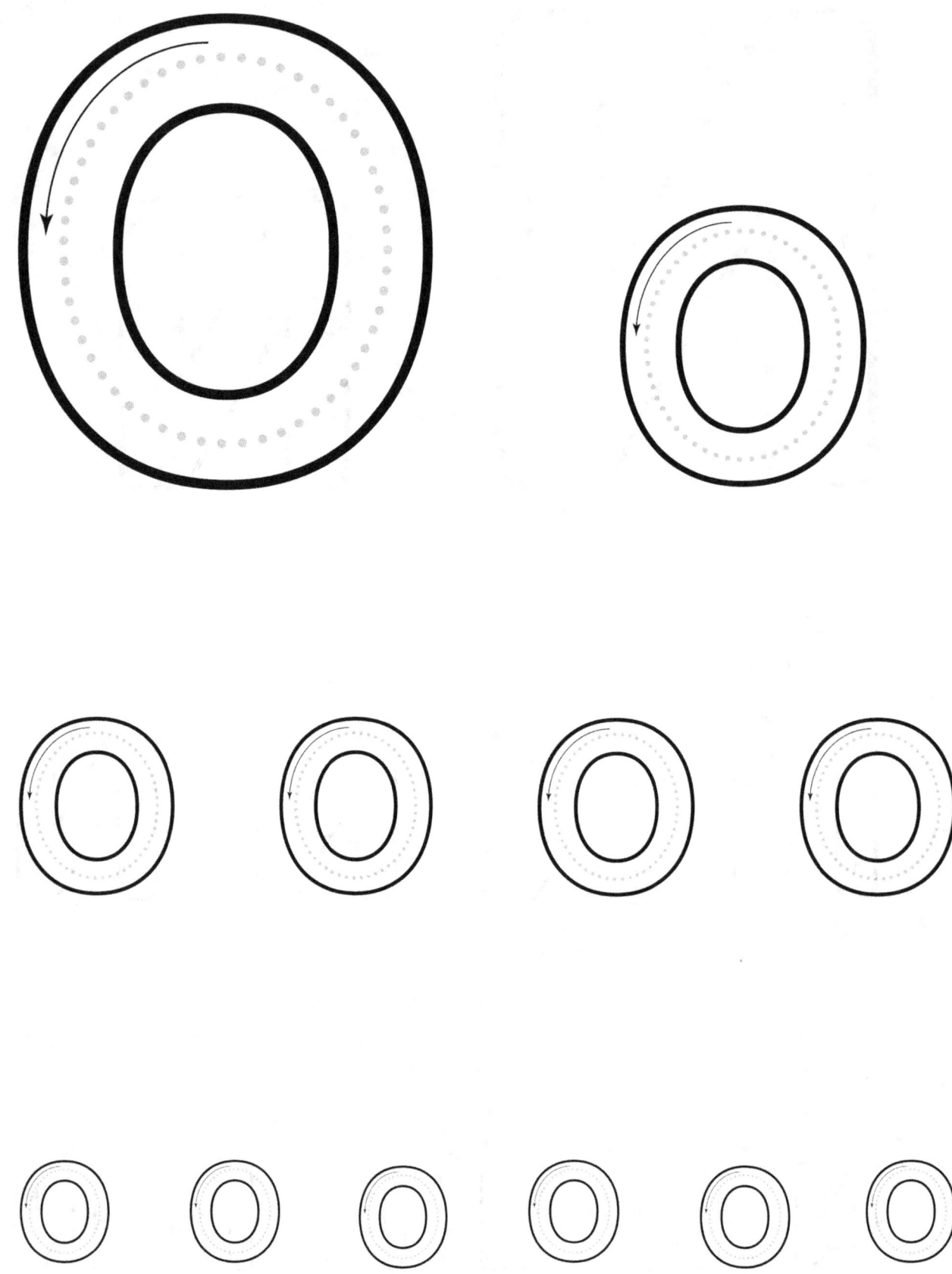

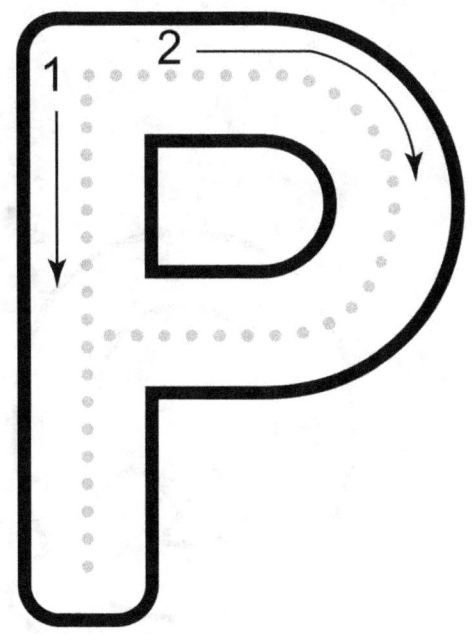
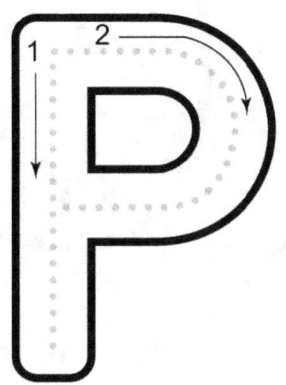
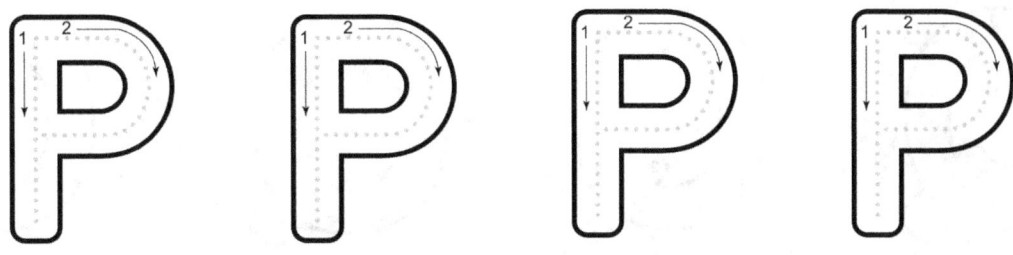

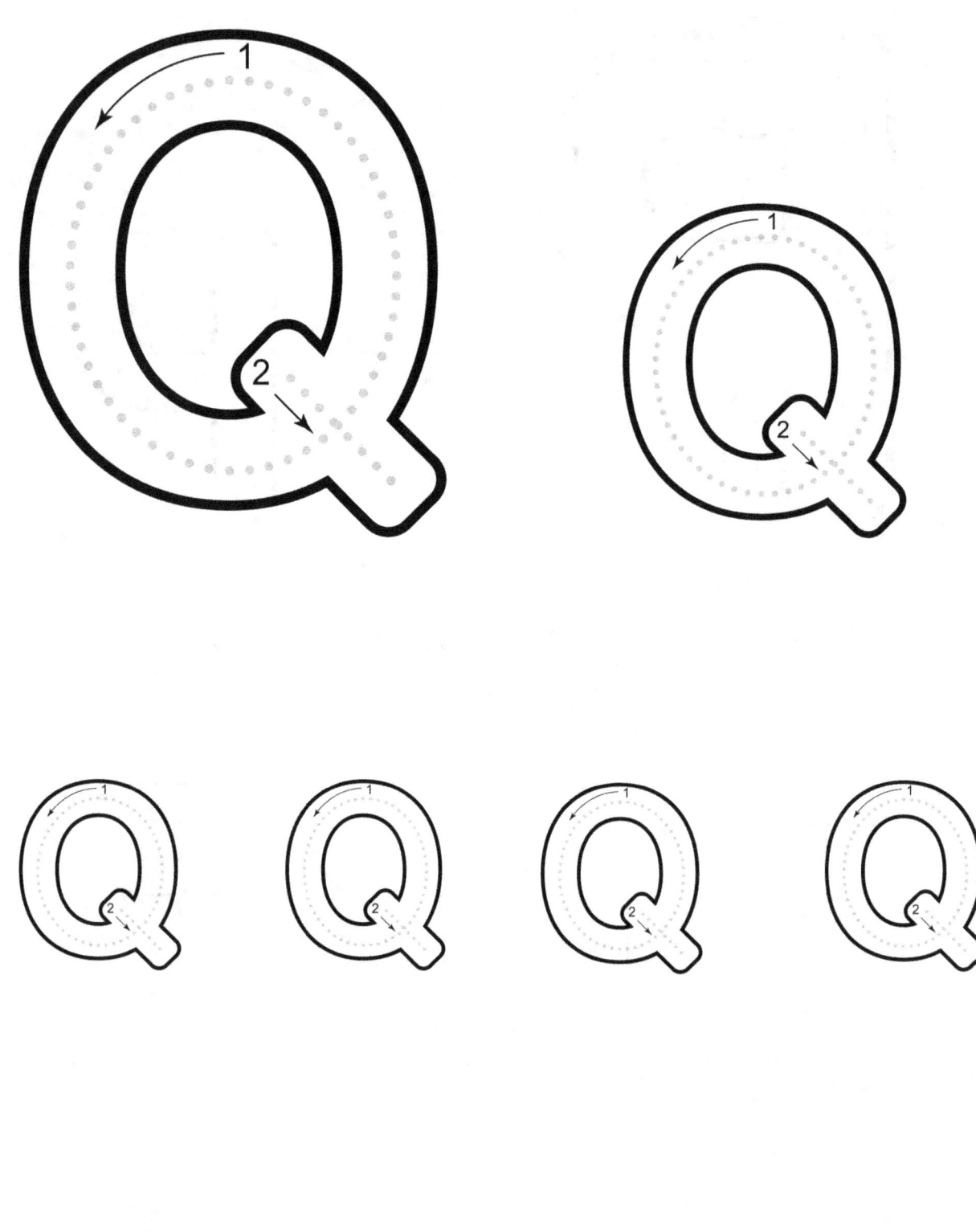

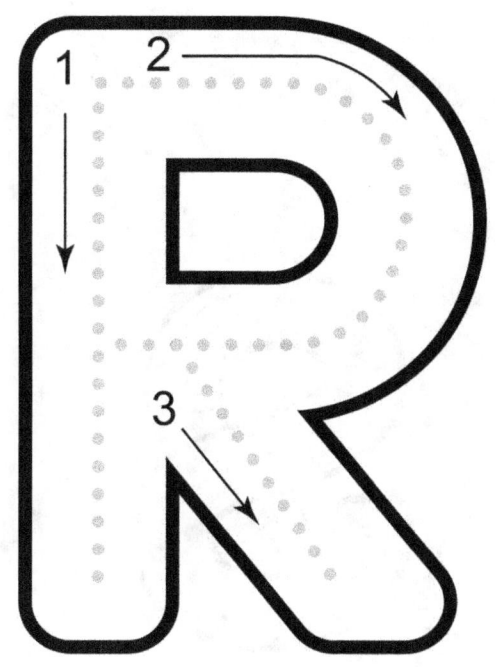
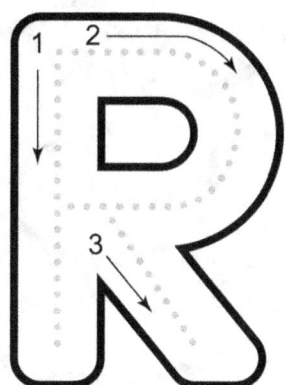

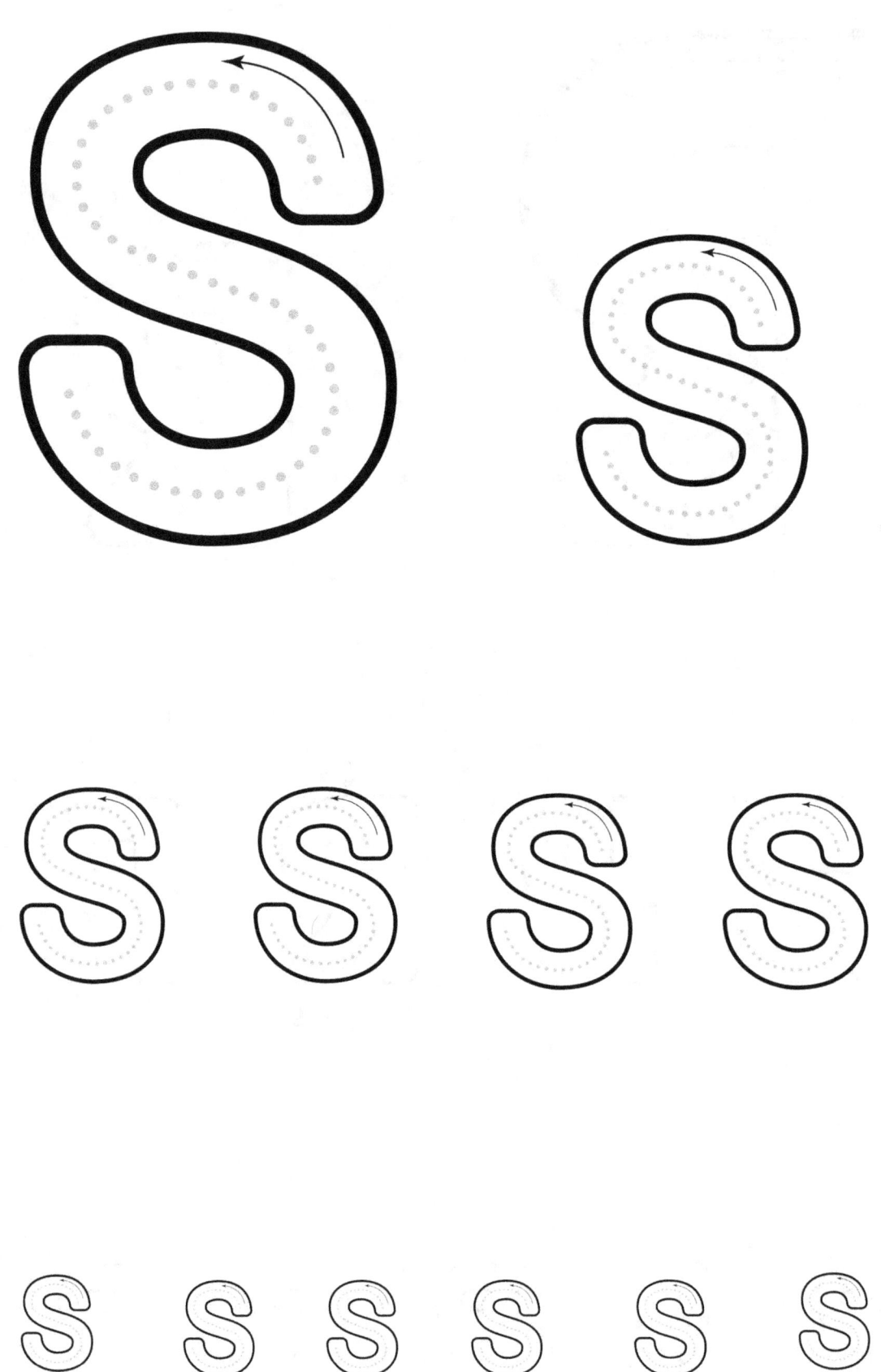

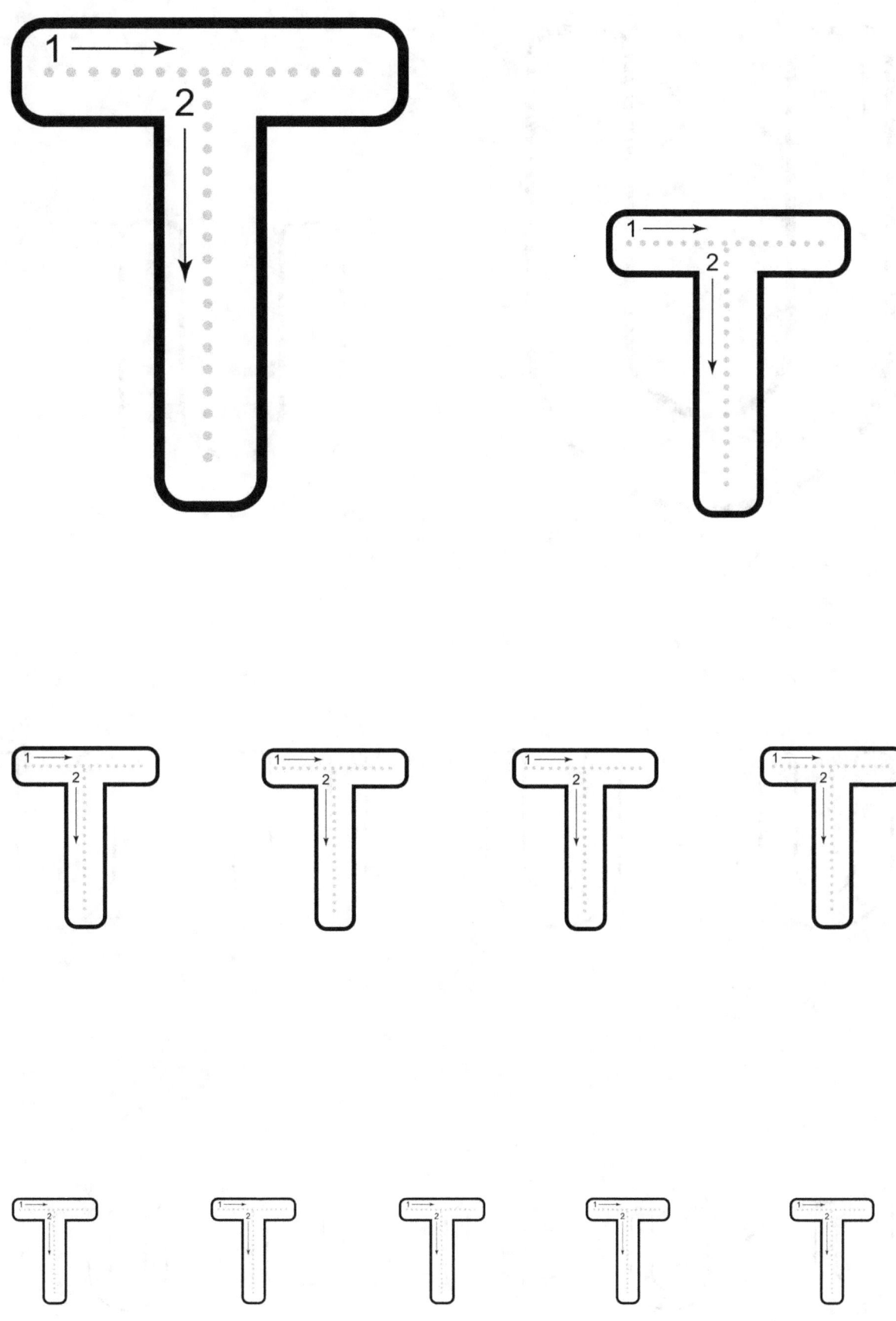

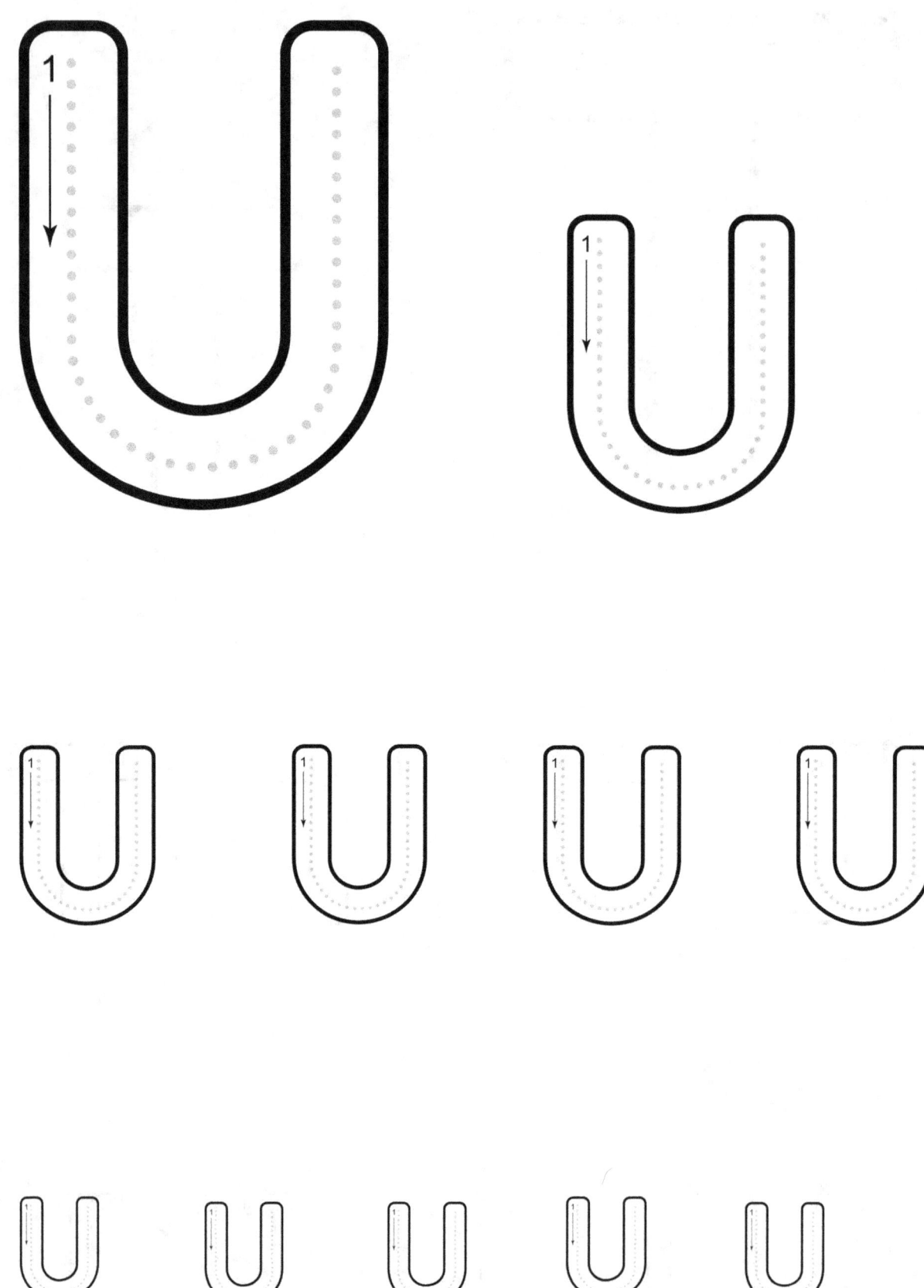

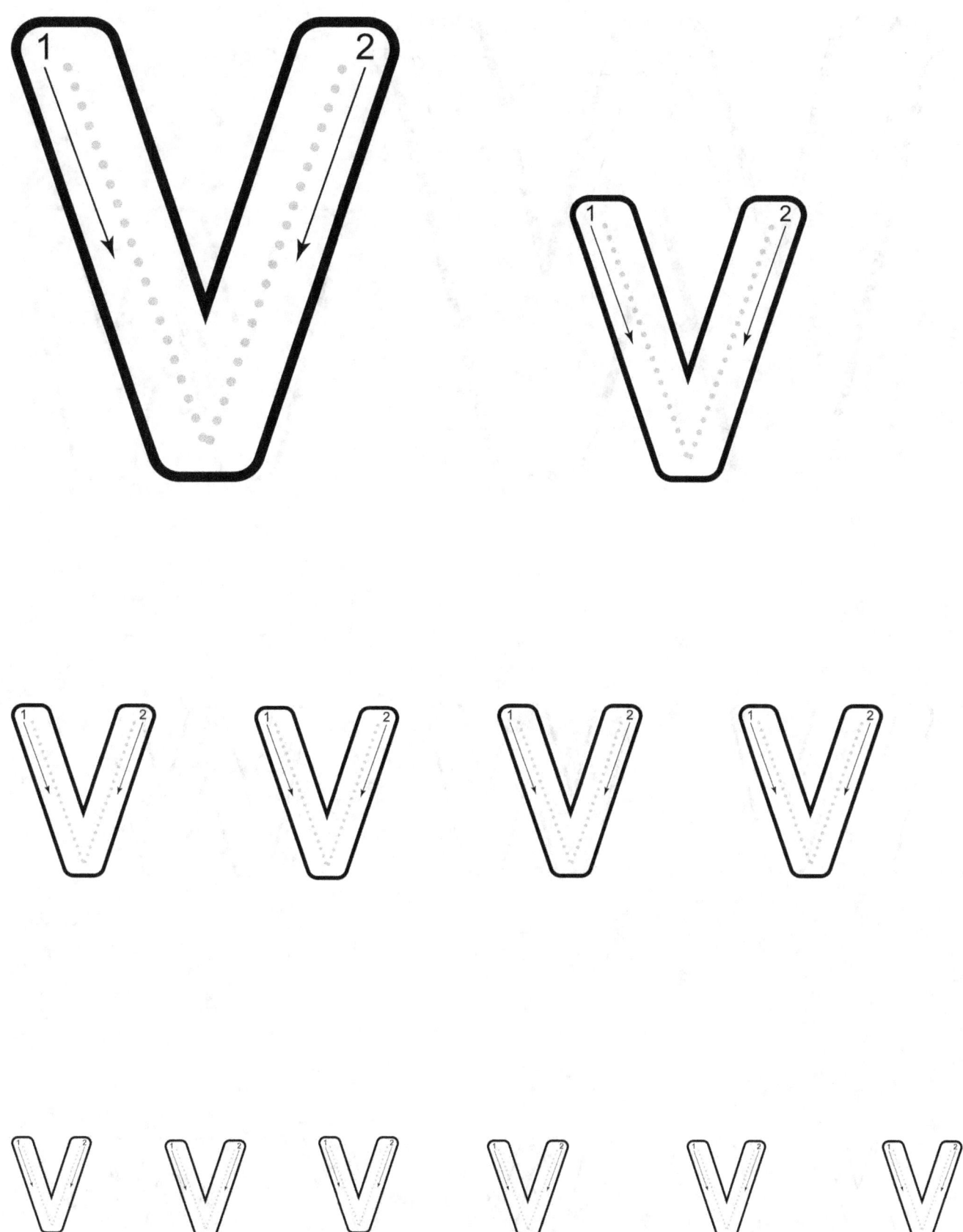

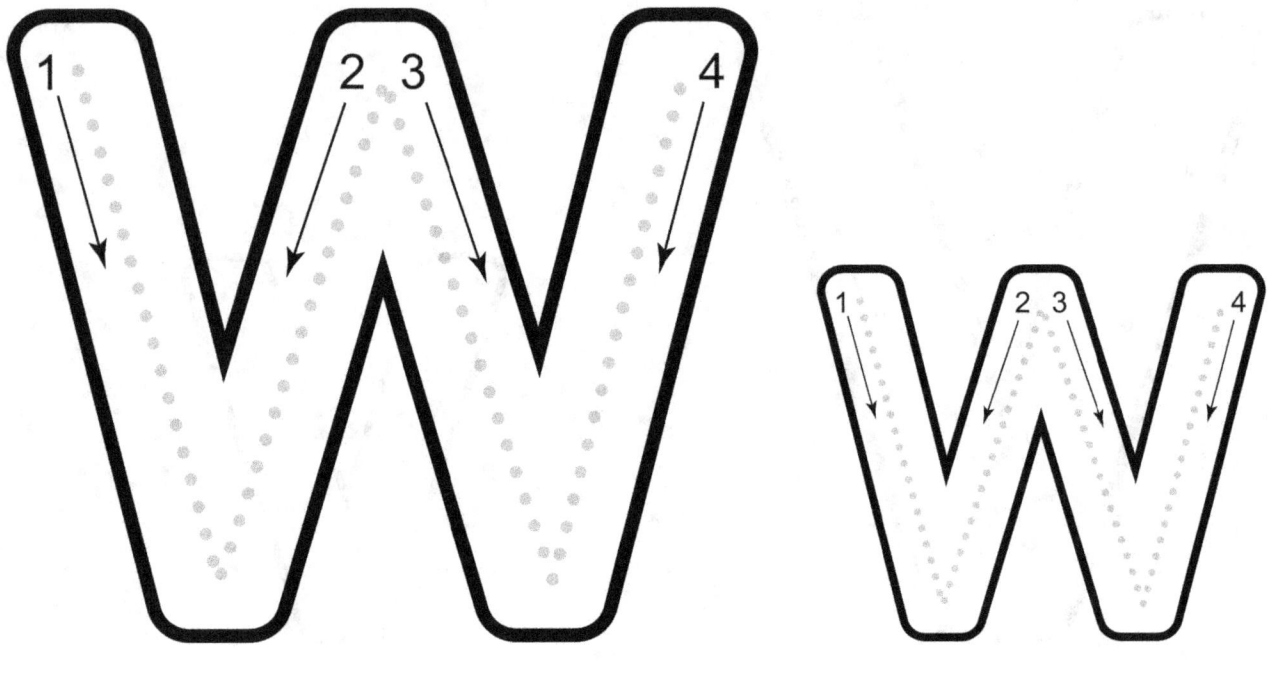

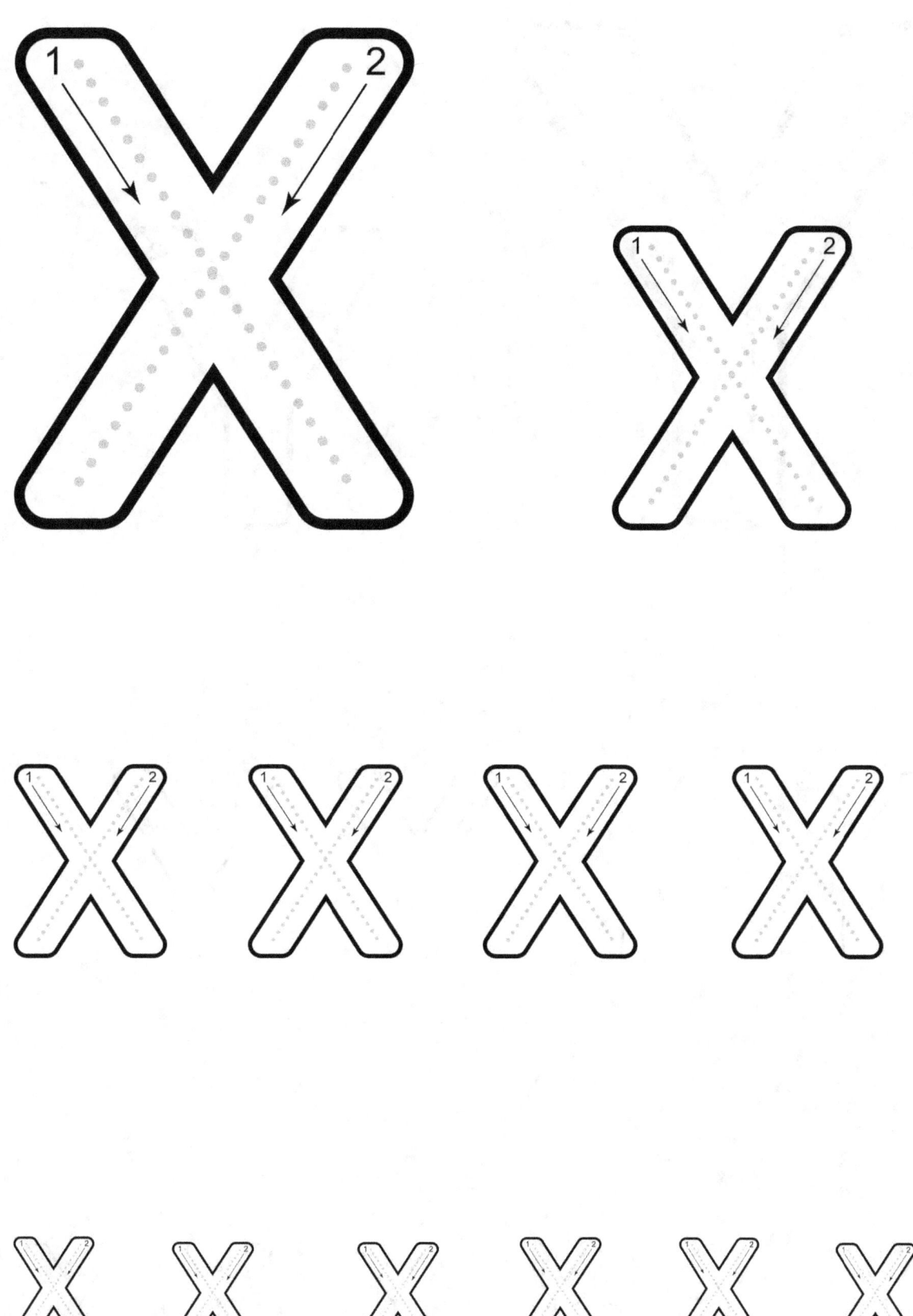

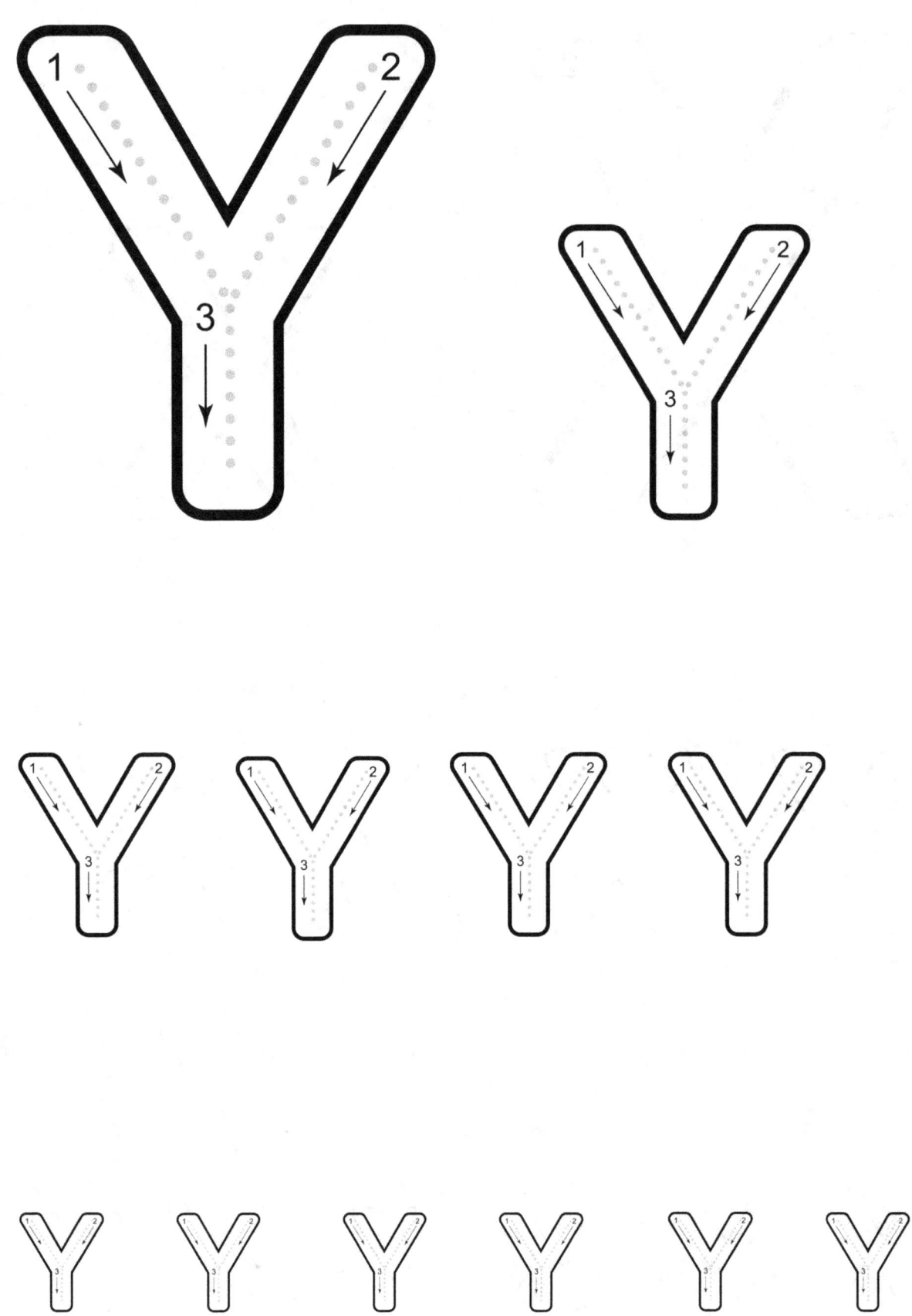

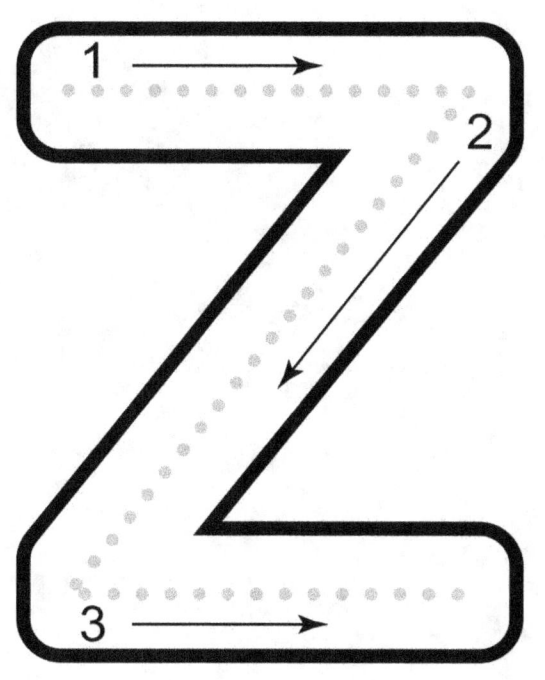
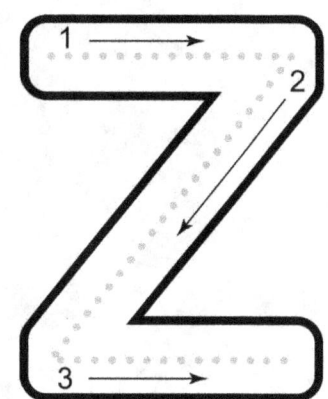
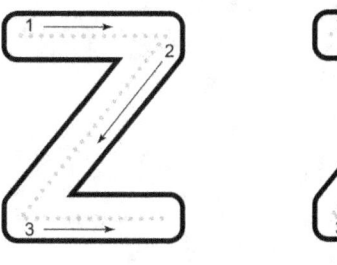
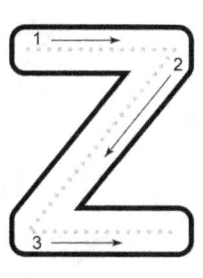
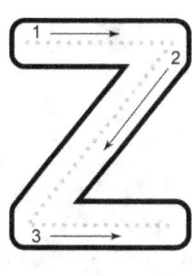
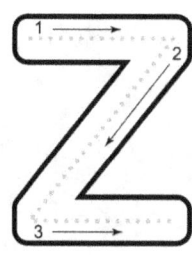

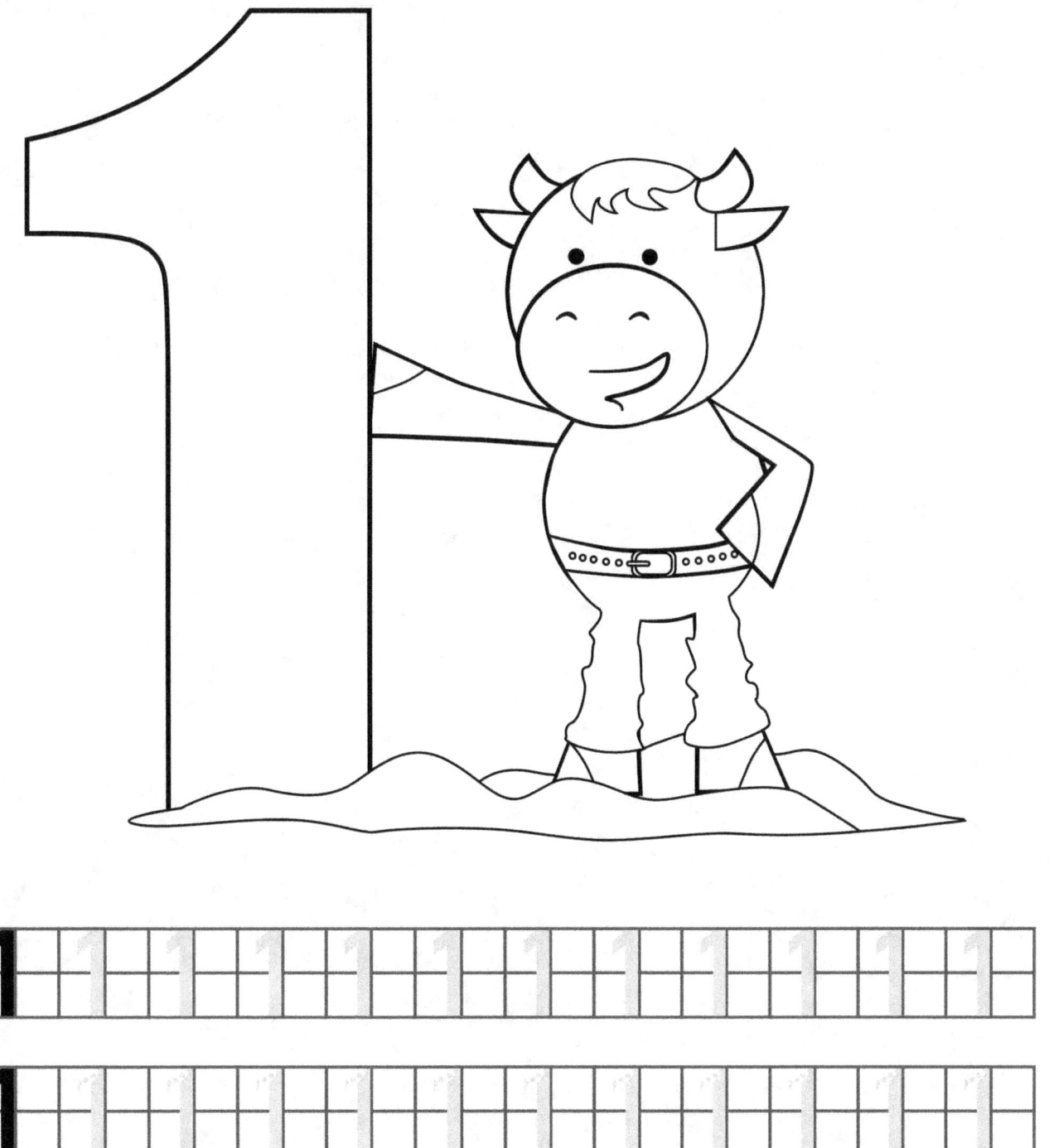

TWO

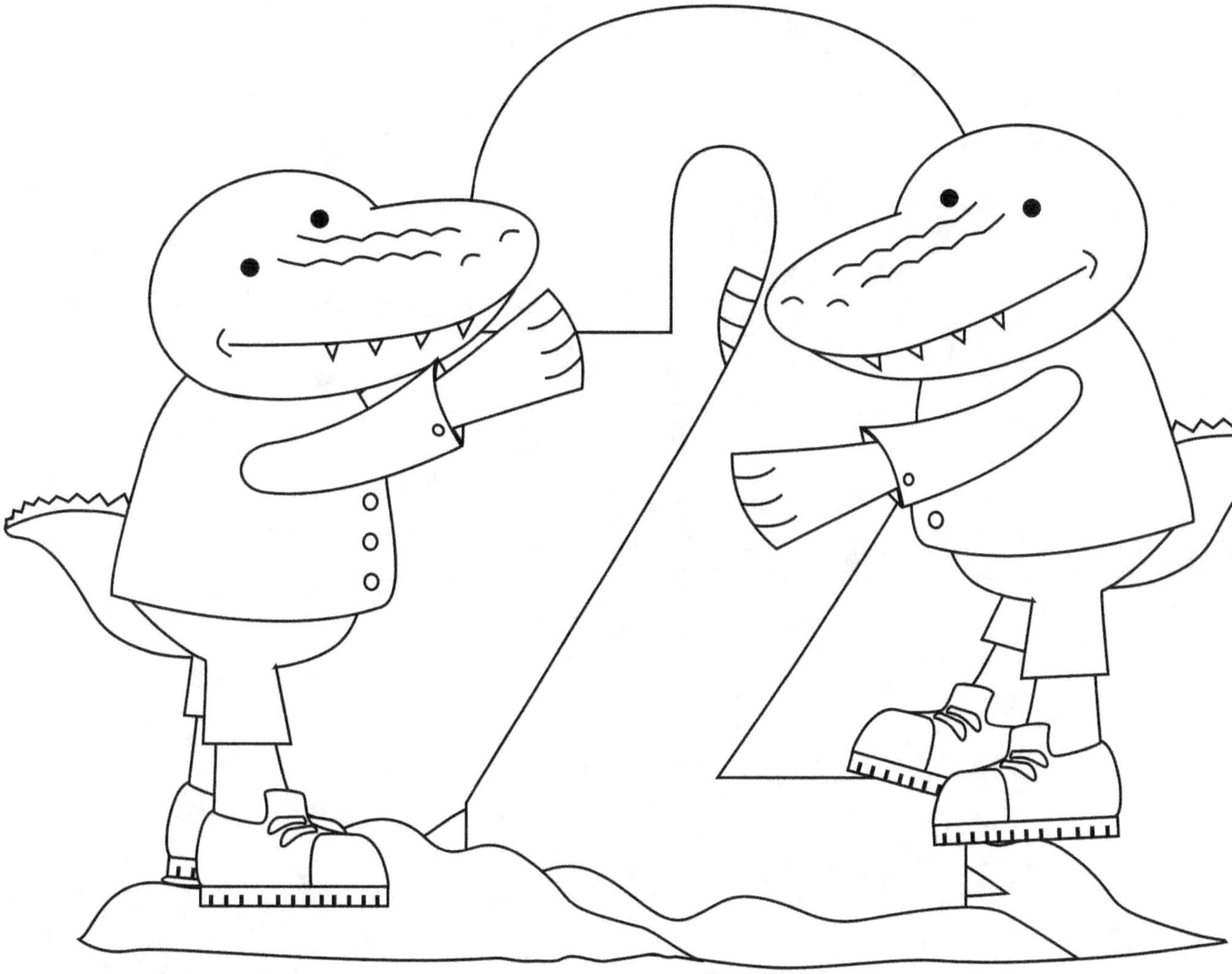

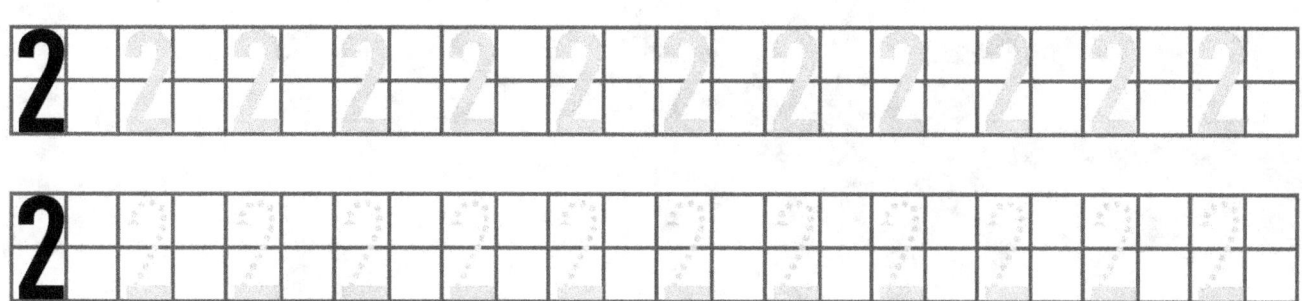

THREE

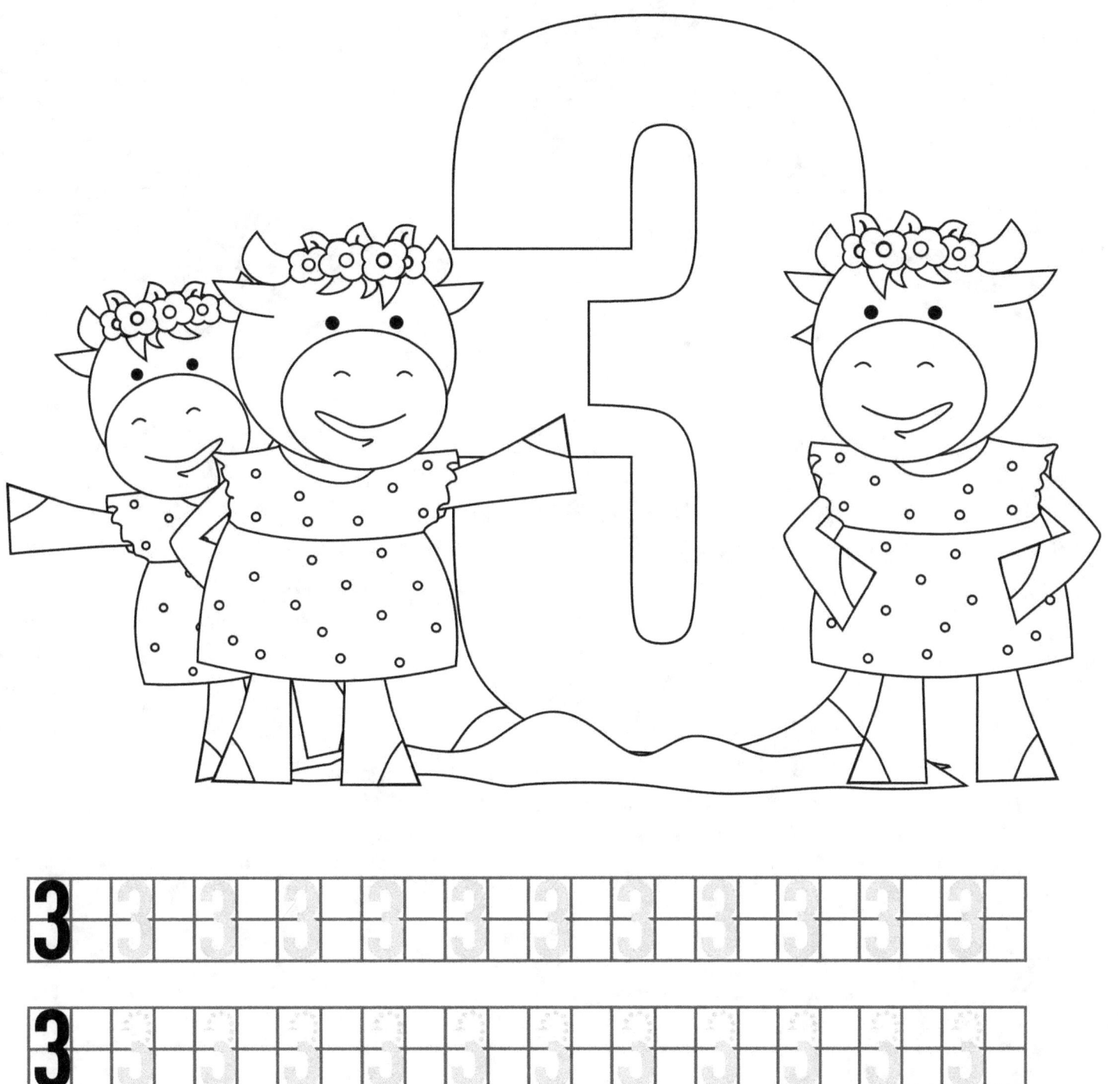

FOUR

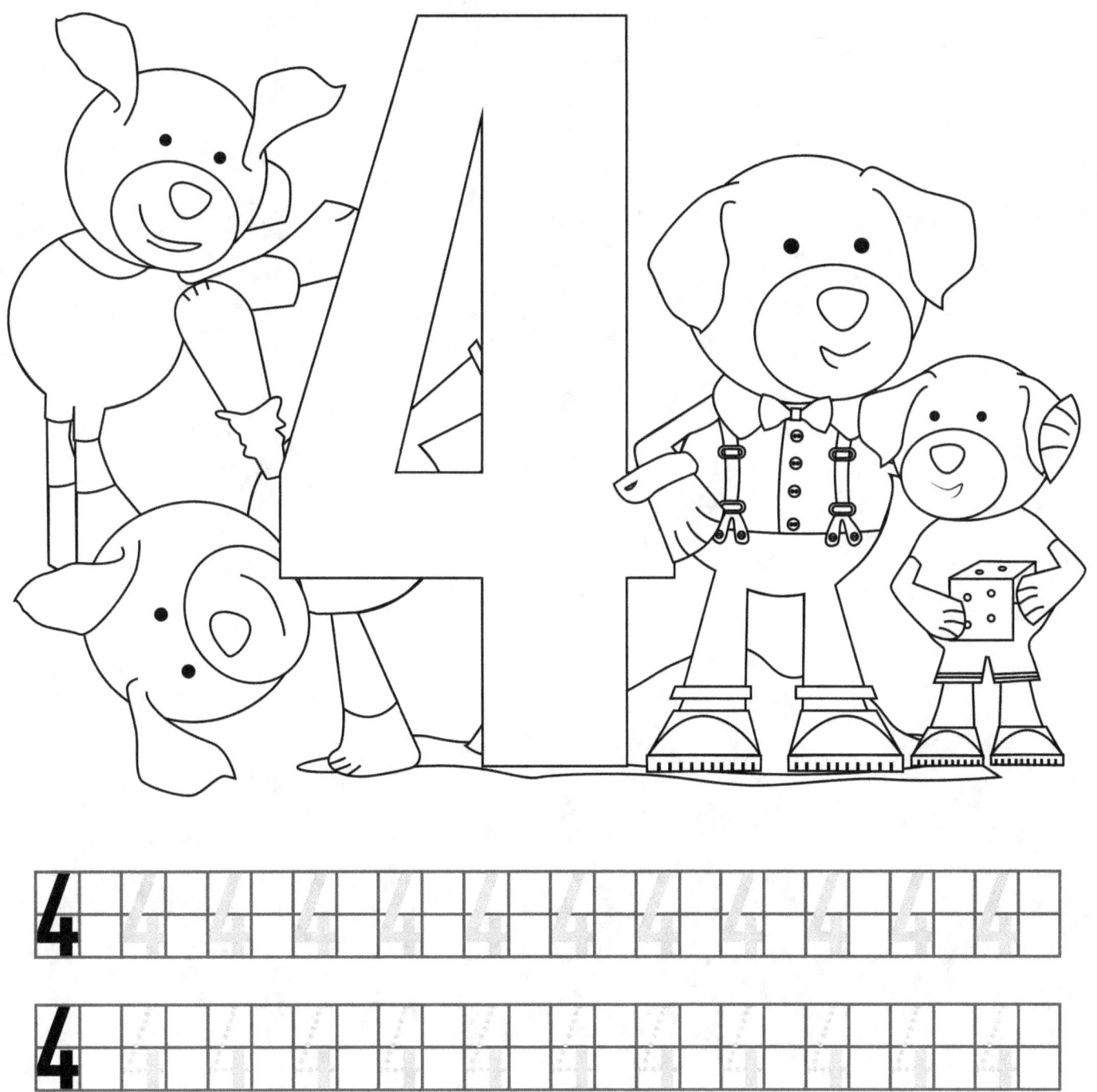

FIVE

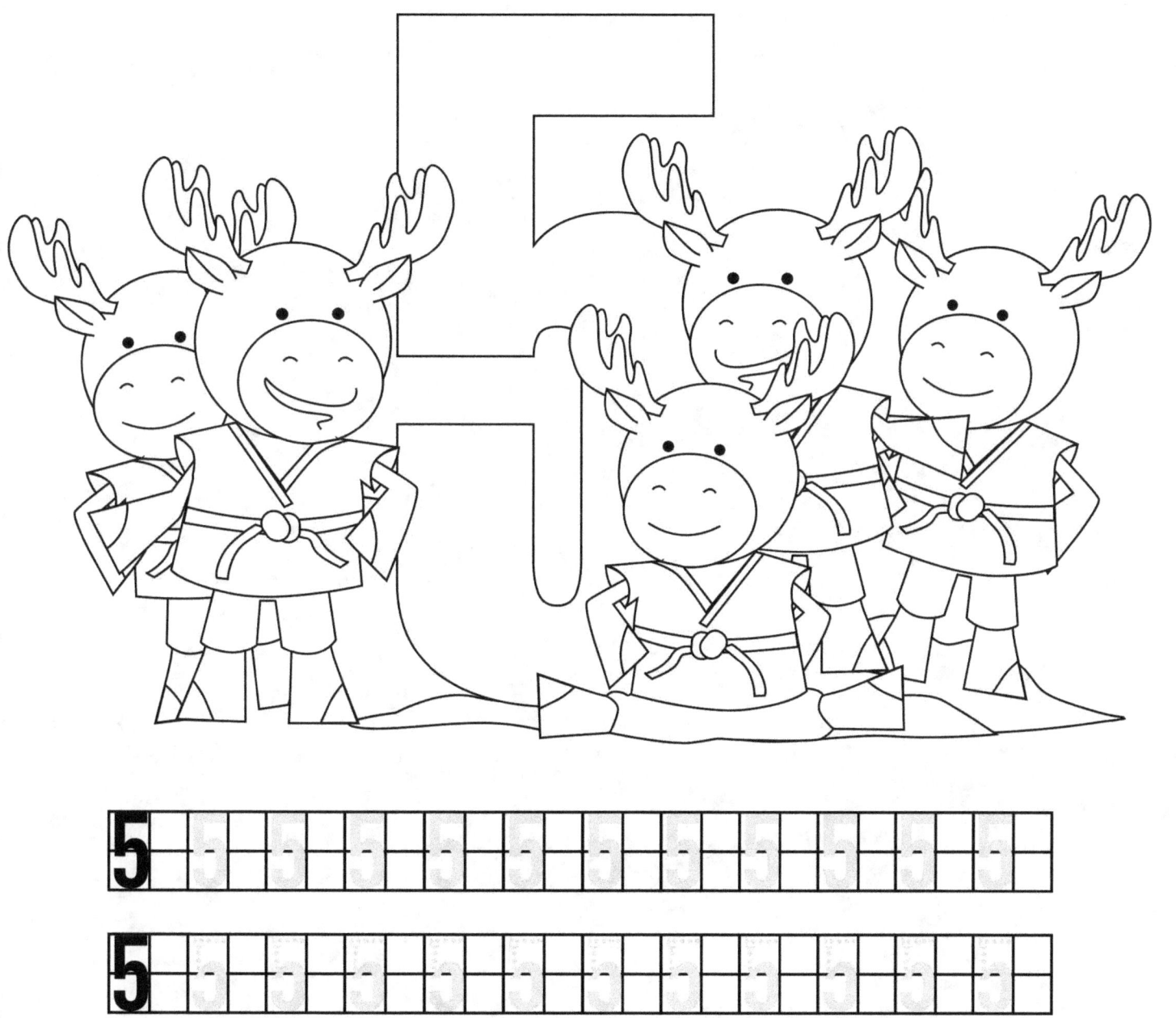

SIX

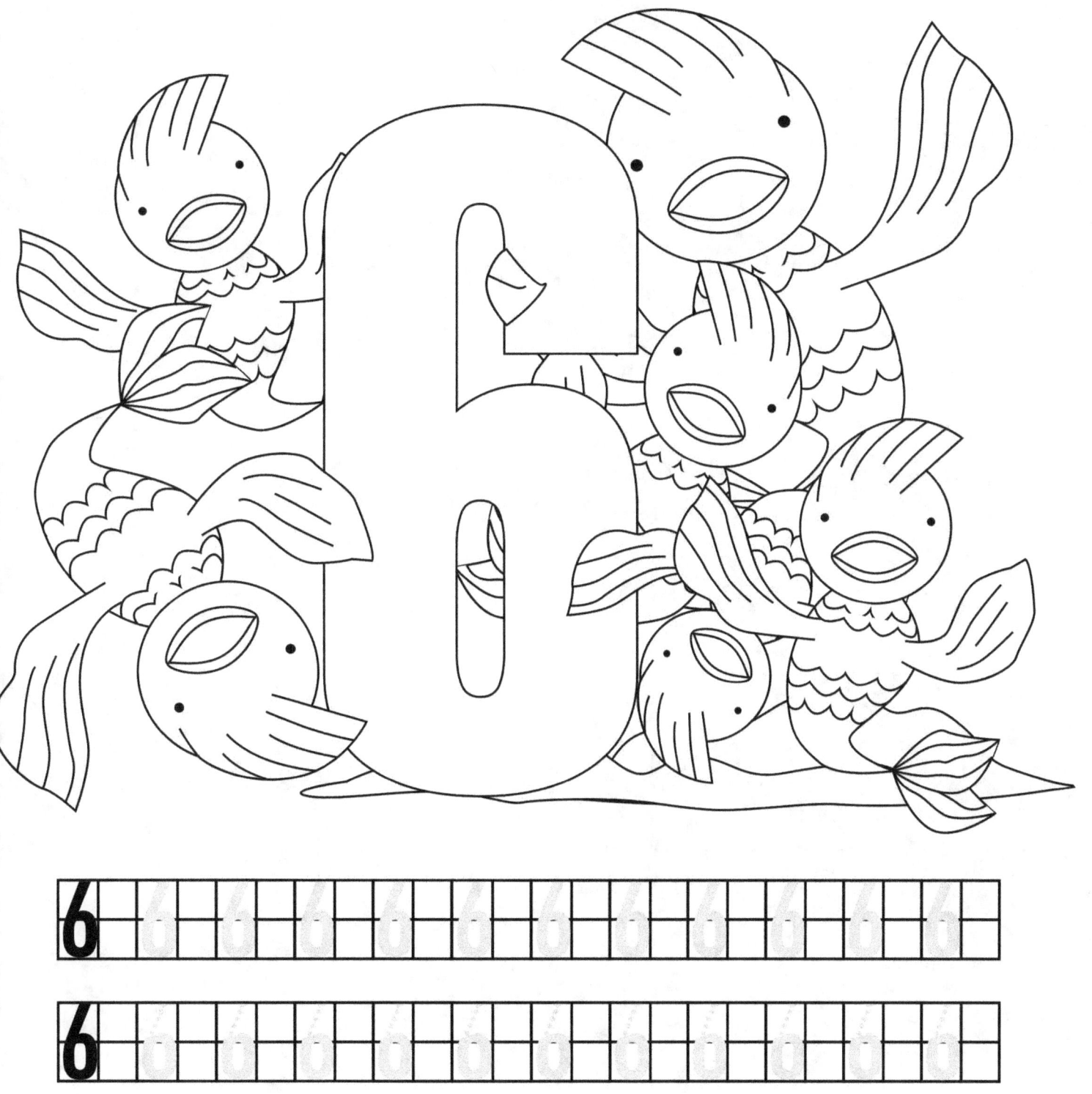

SEVEN

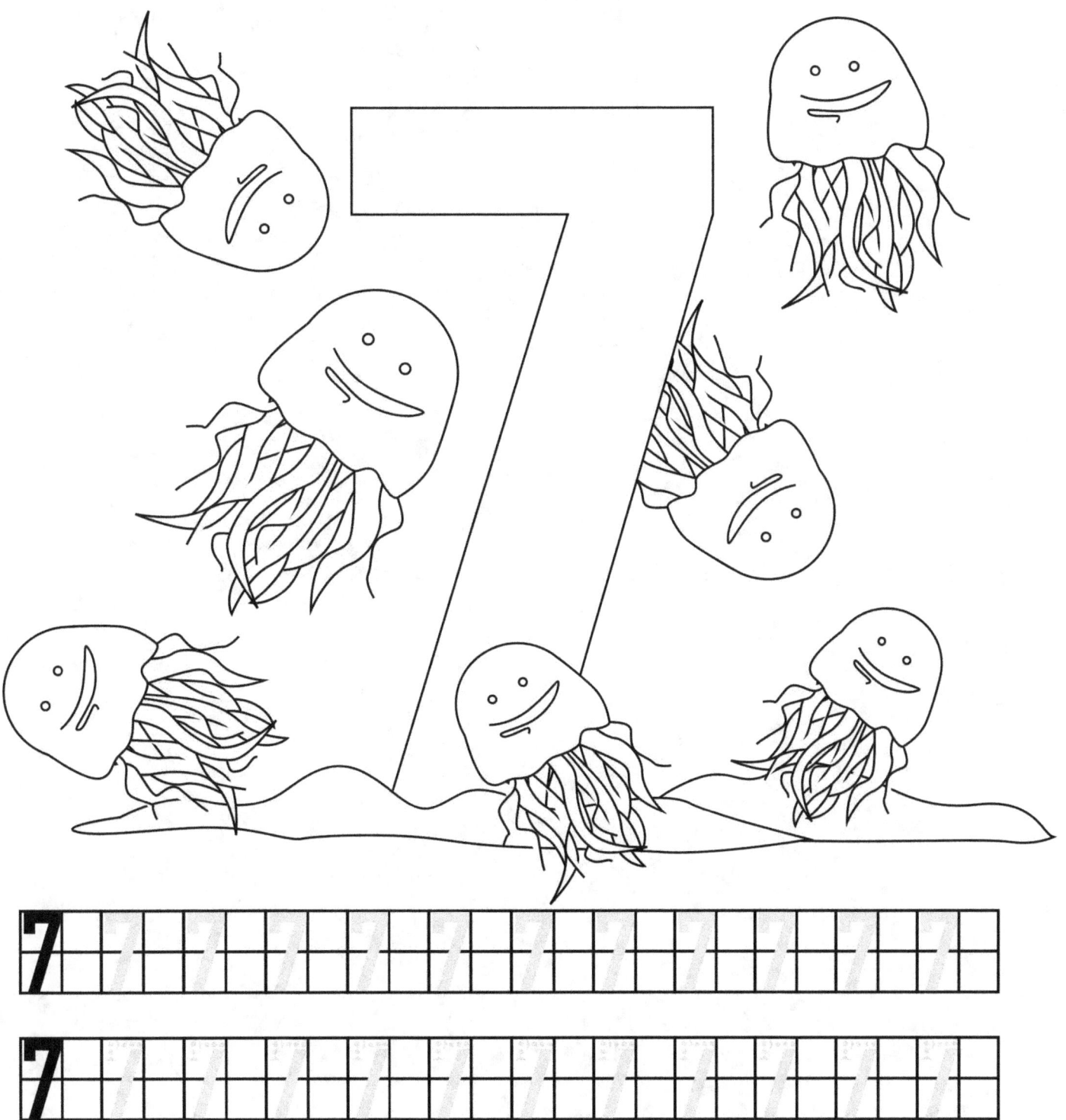

EIGHT

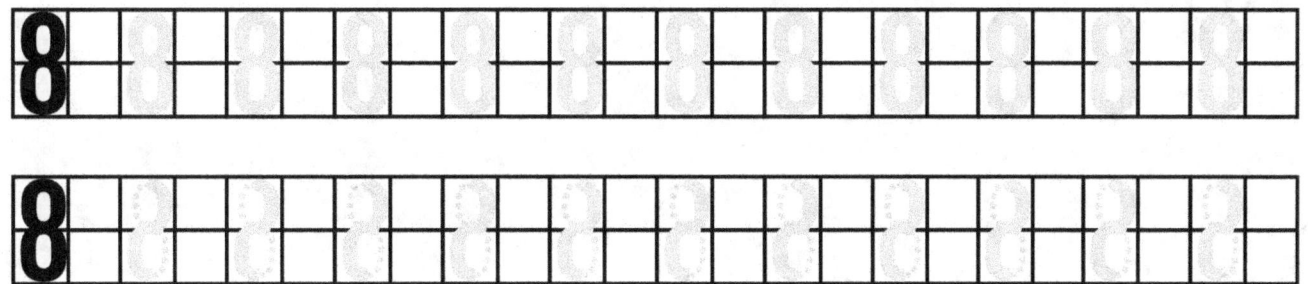

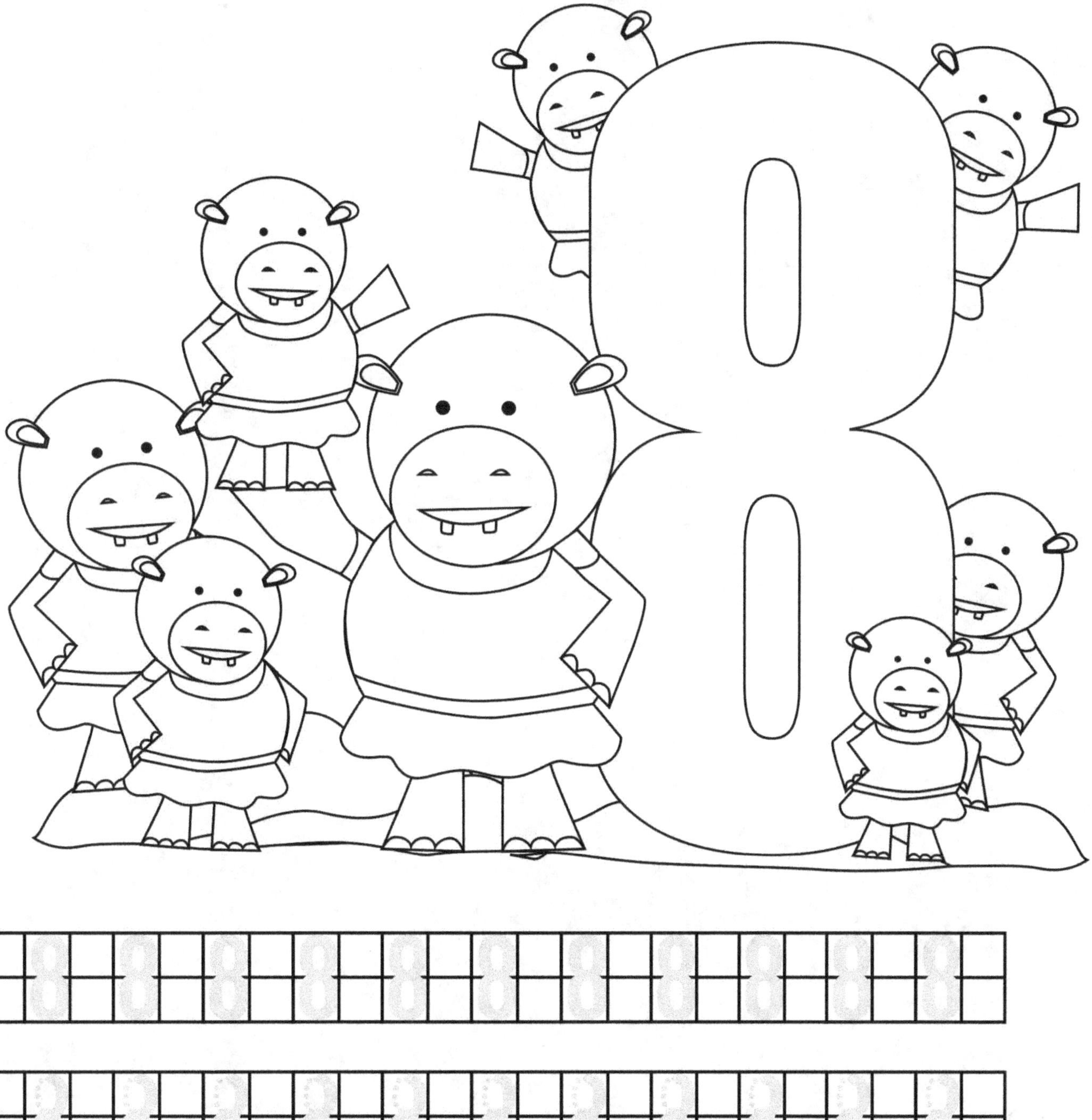

NINE

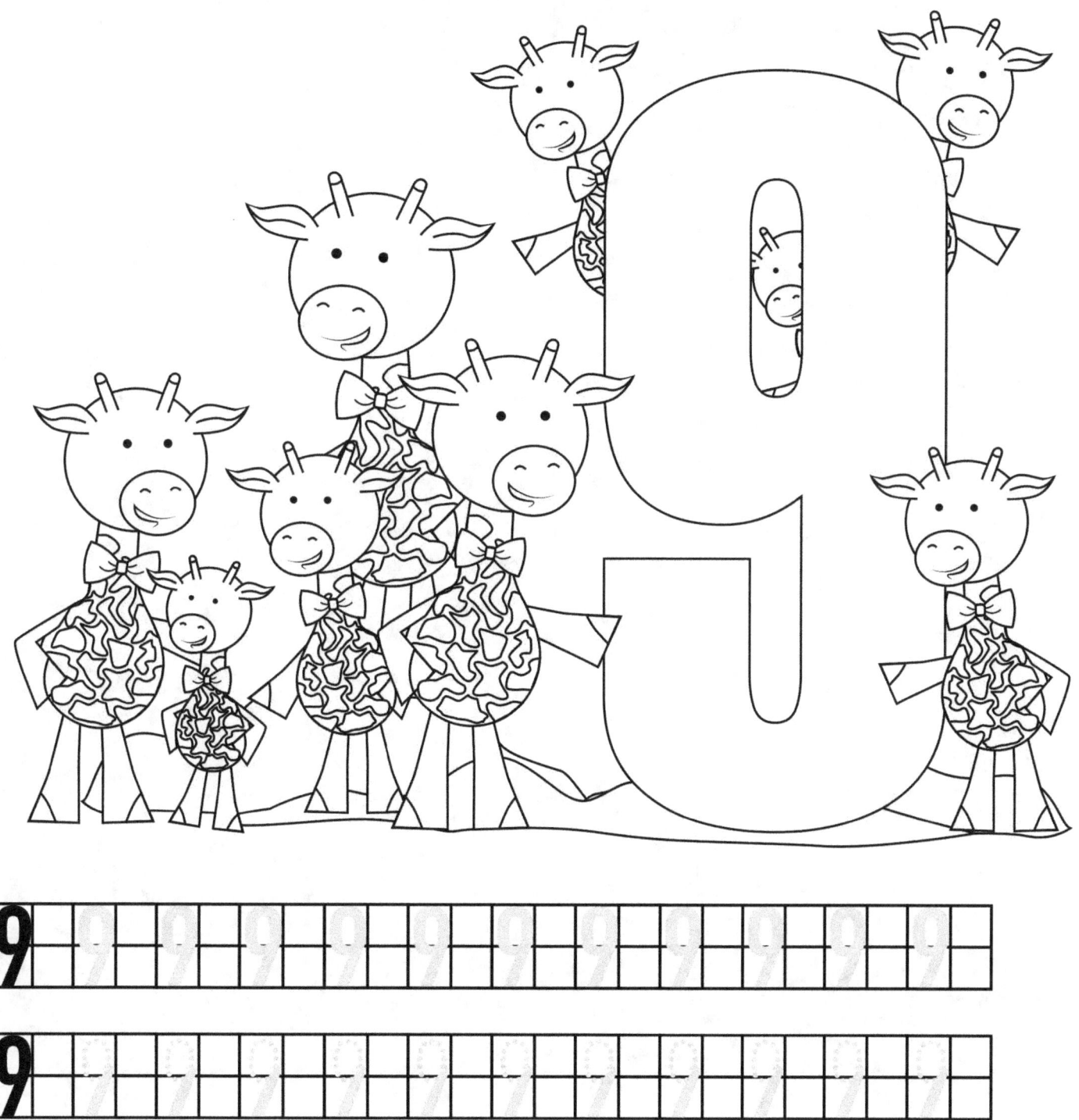

Find the way

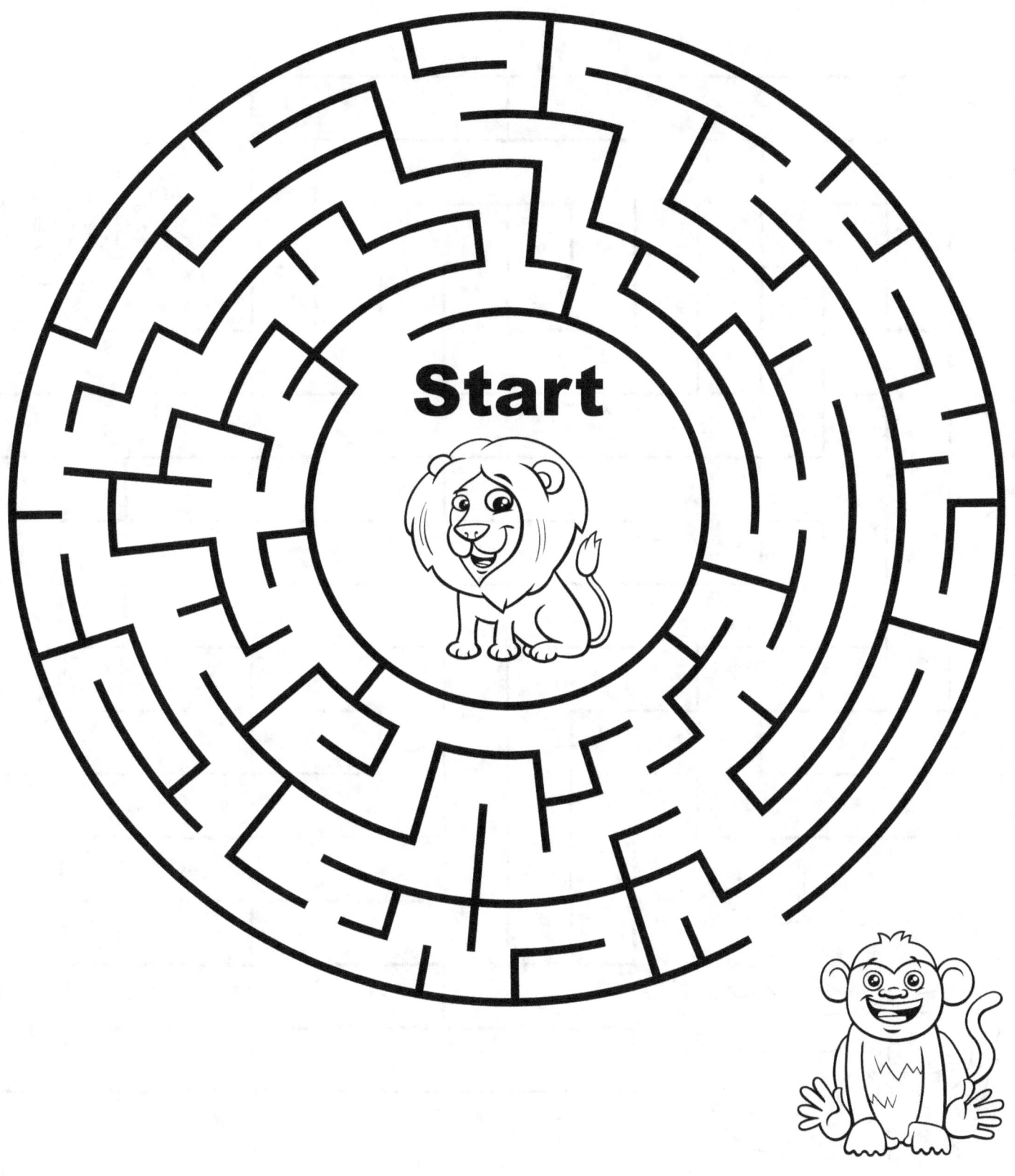

Find the way

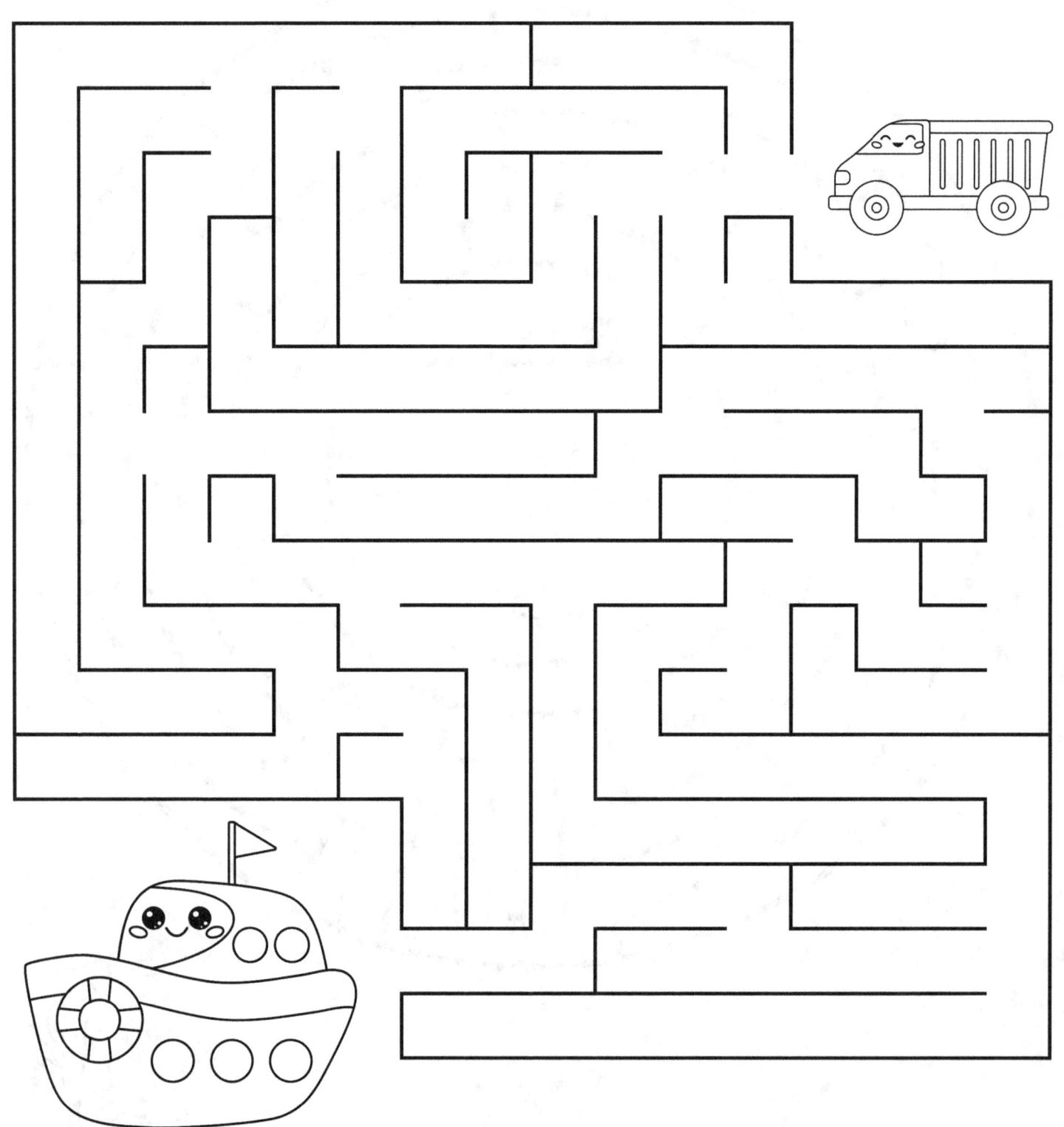

Find the way

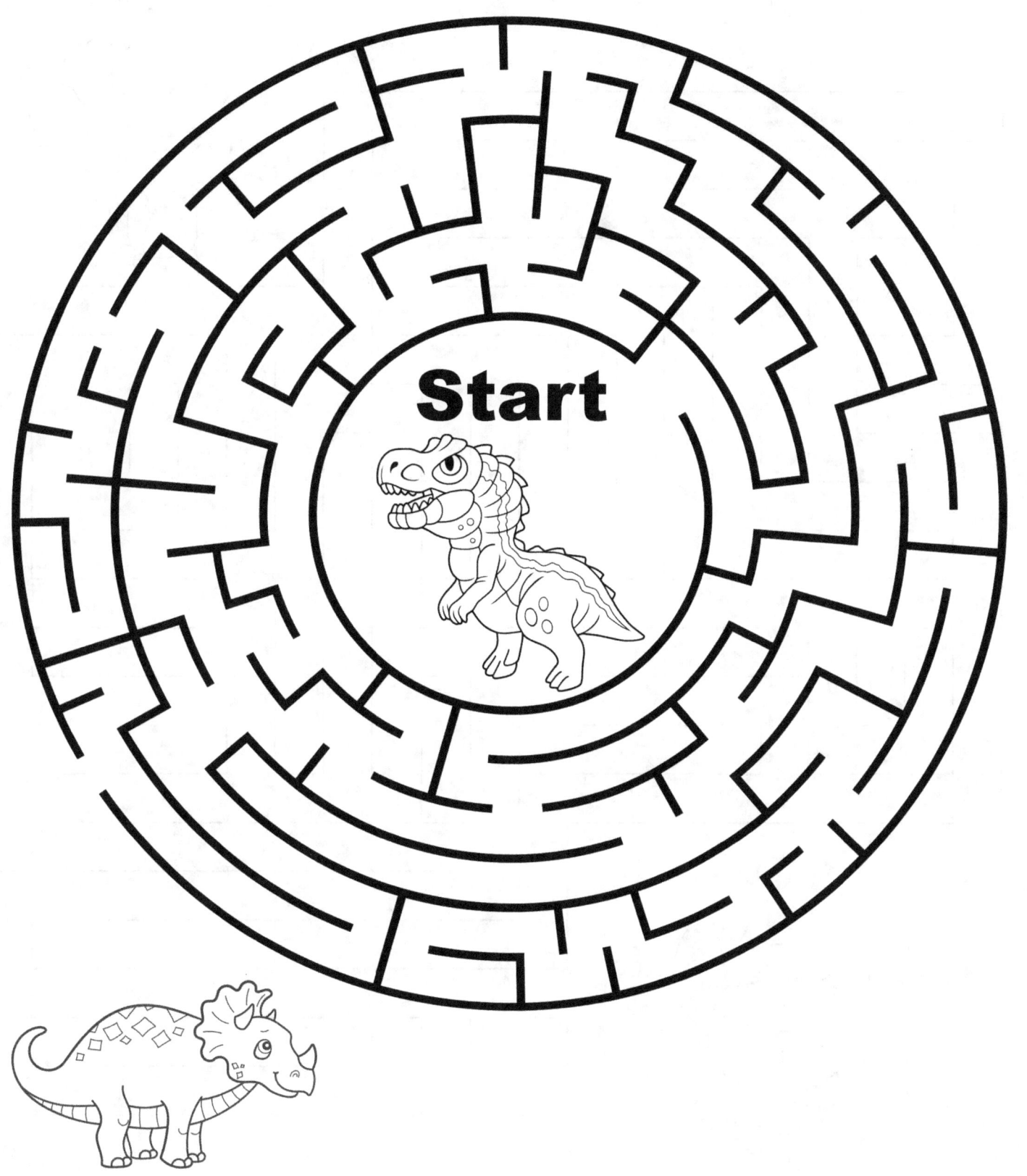

Find the way

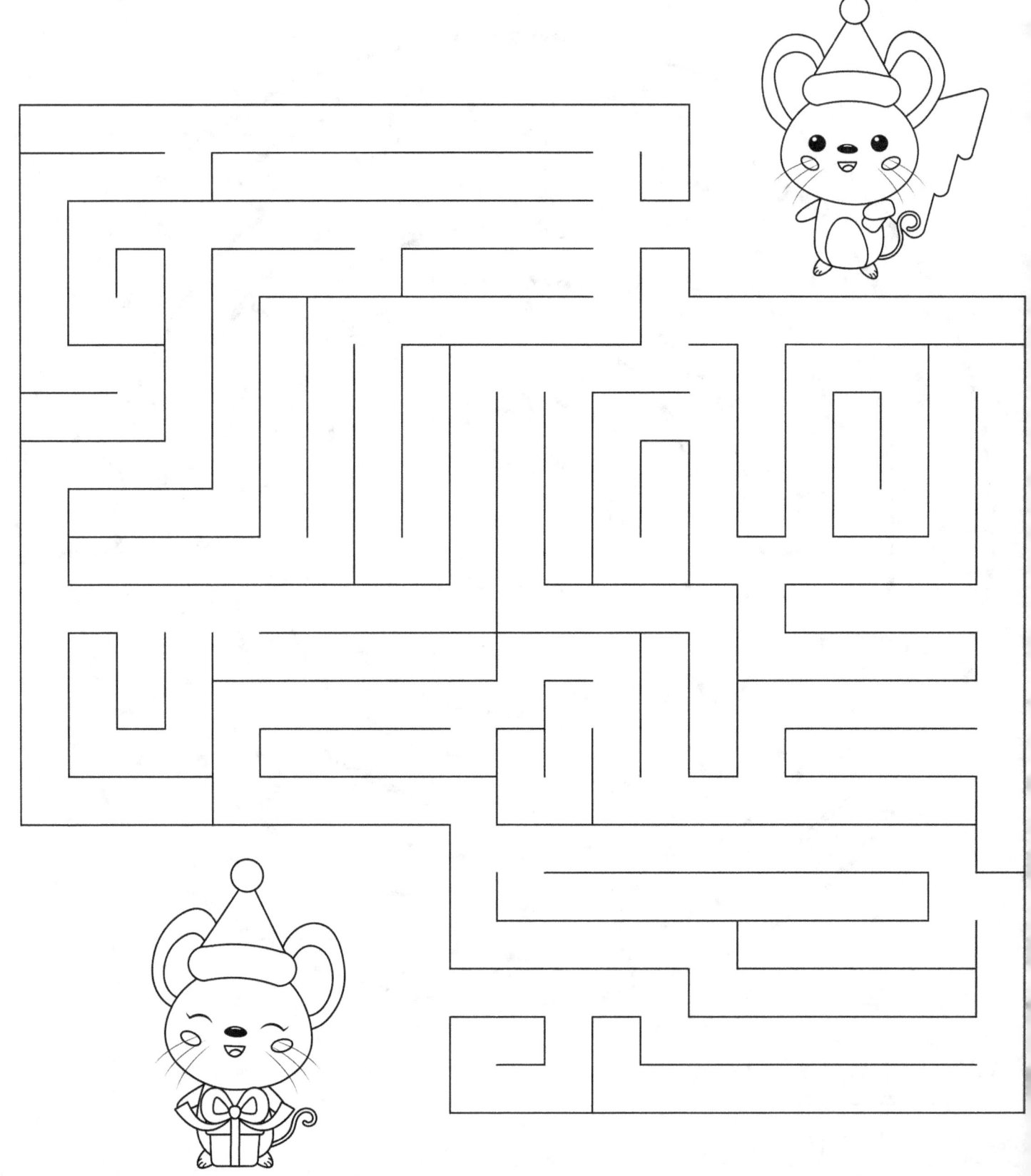

Find the way

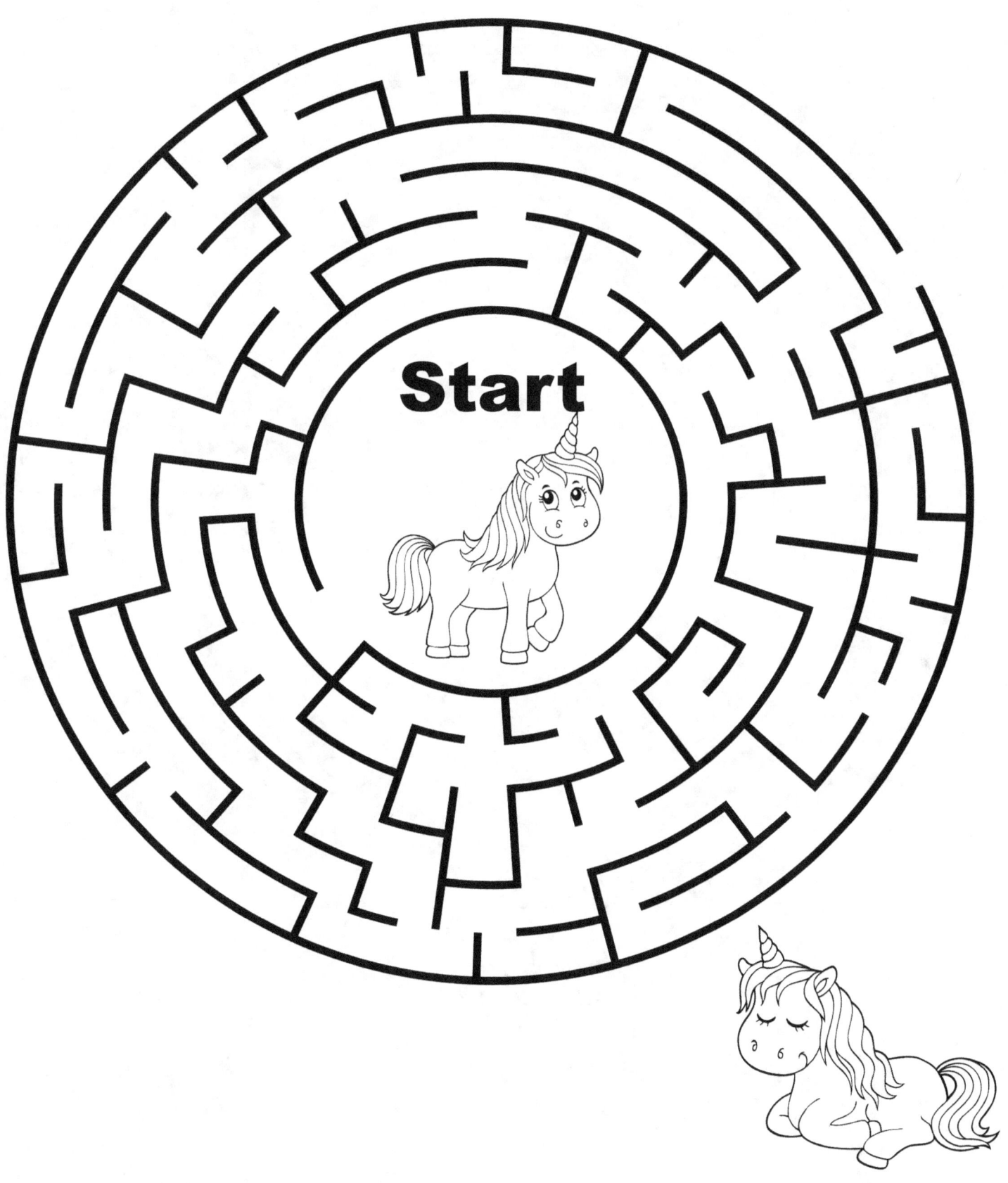

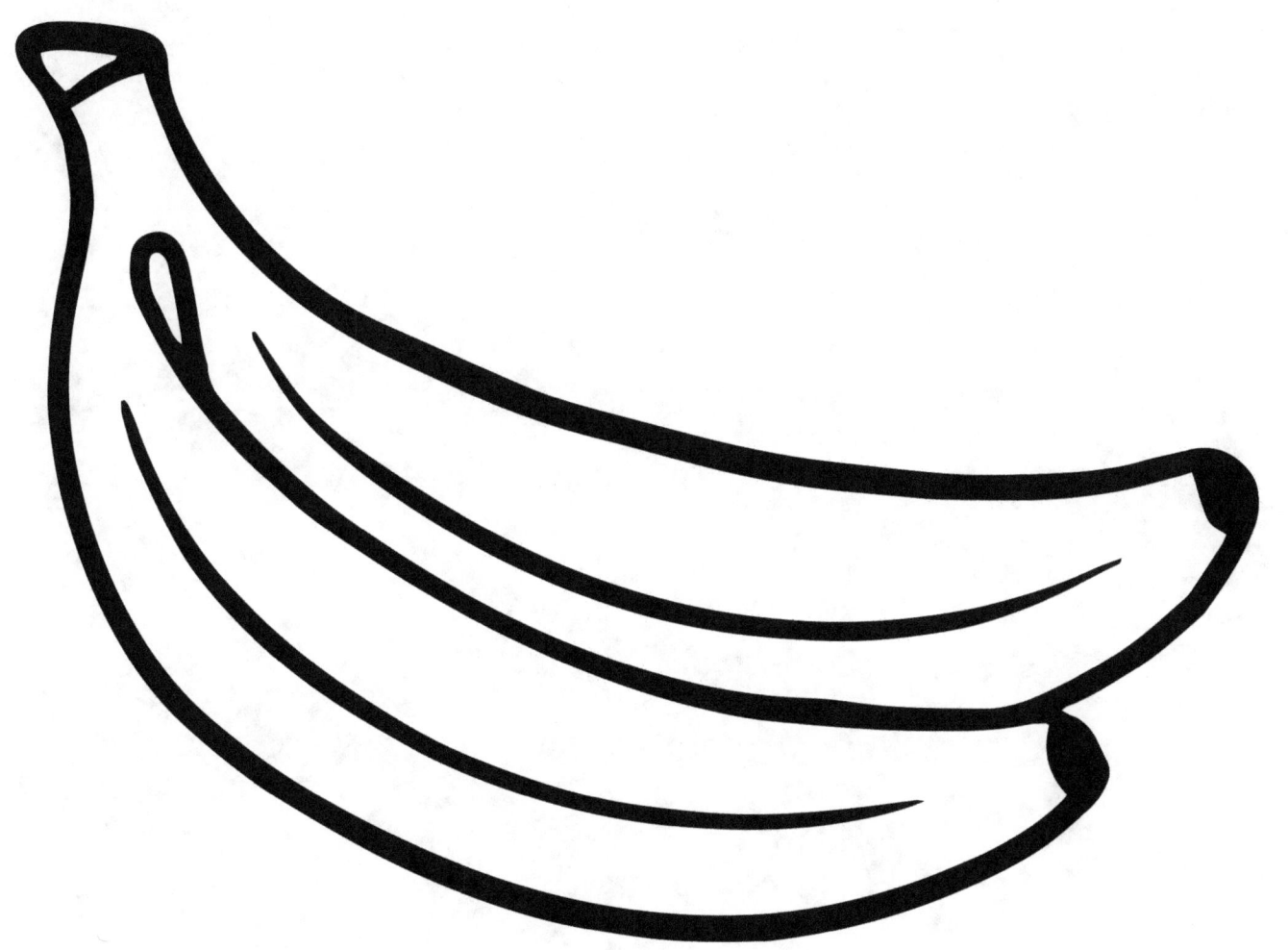

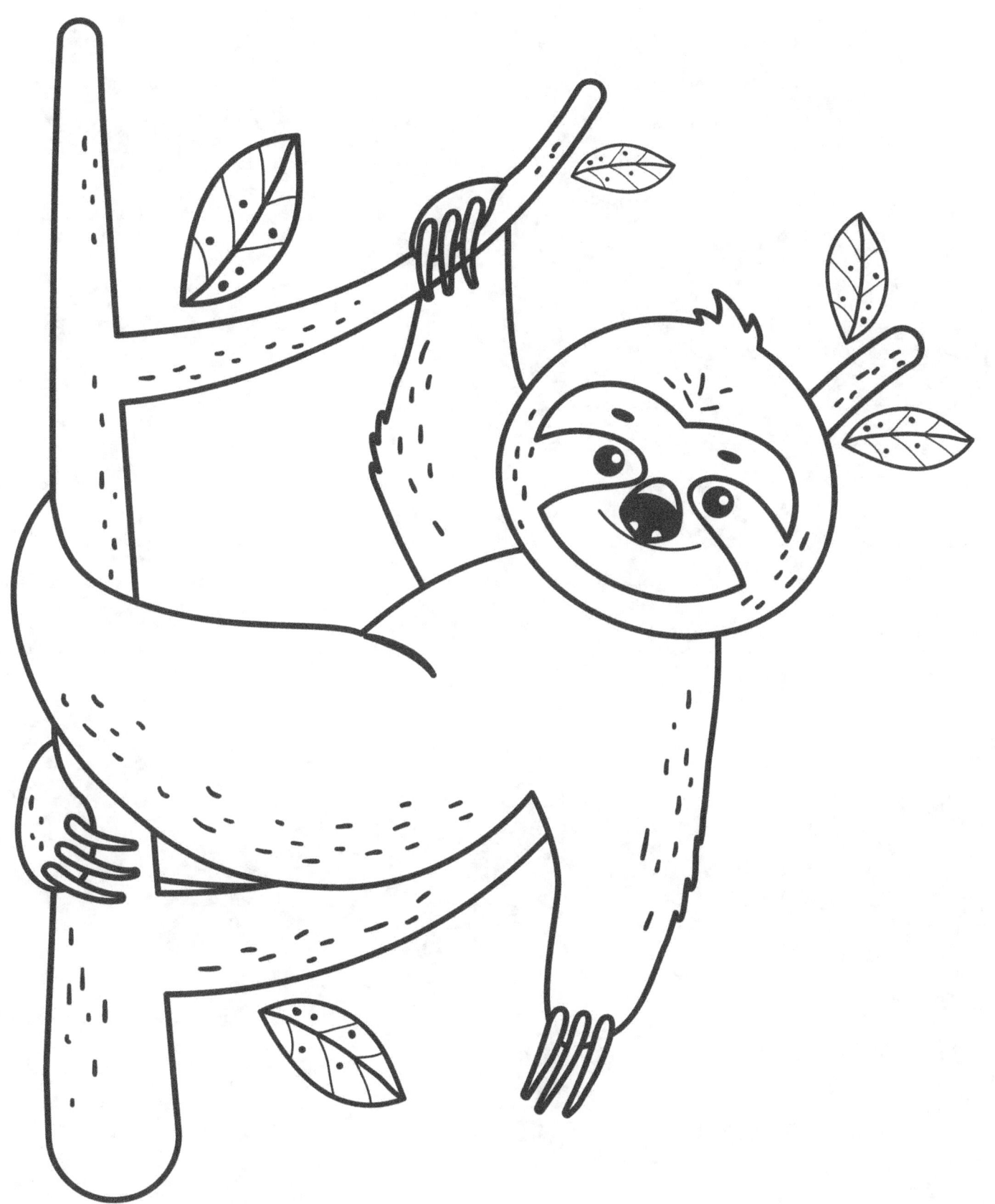

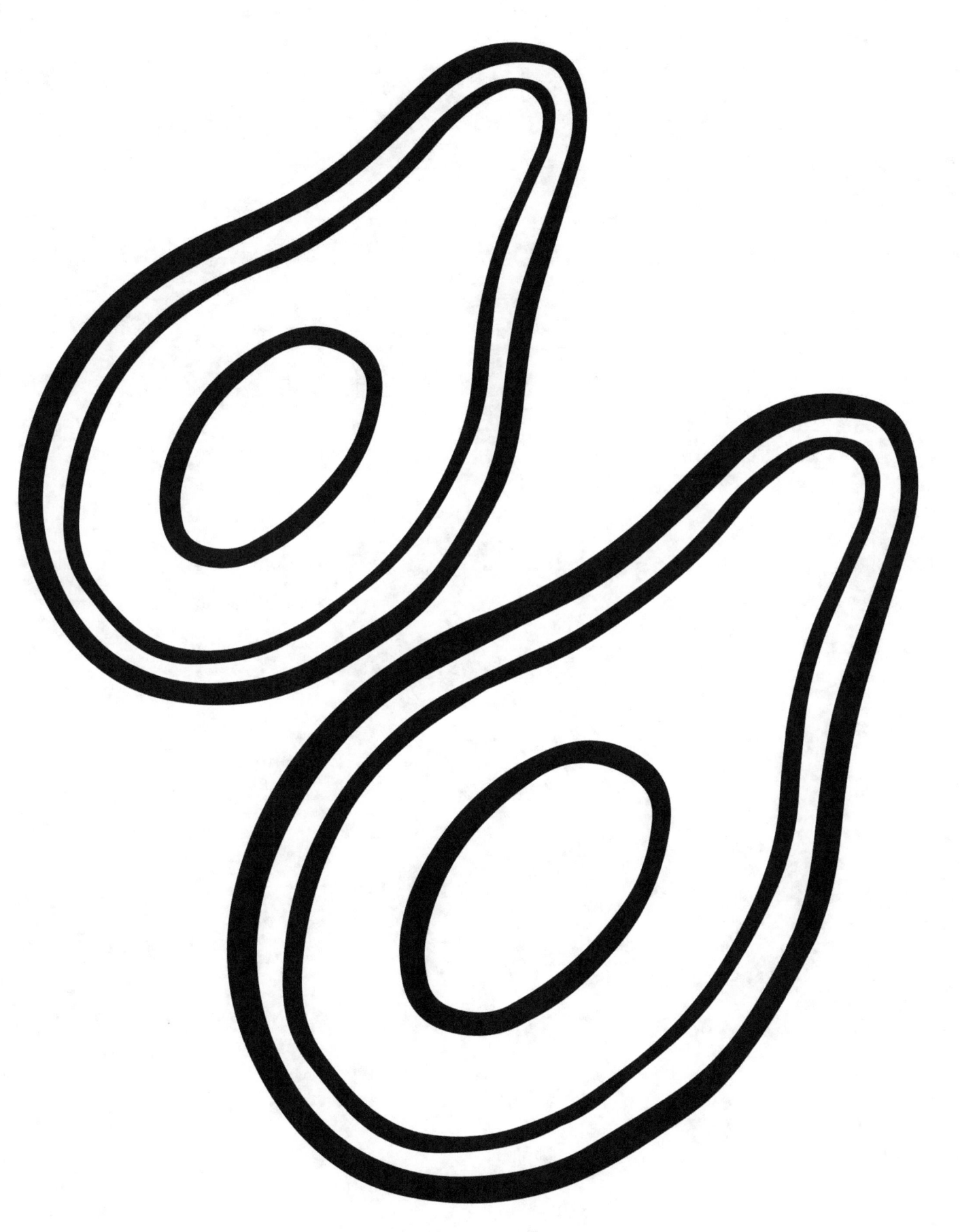

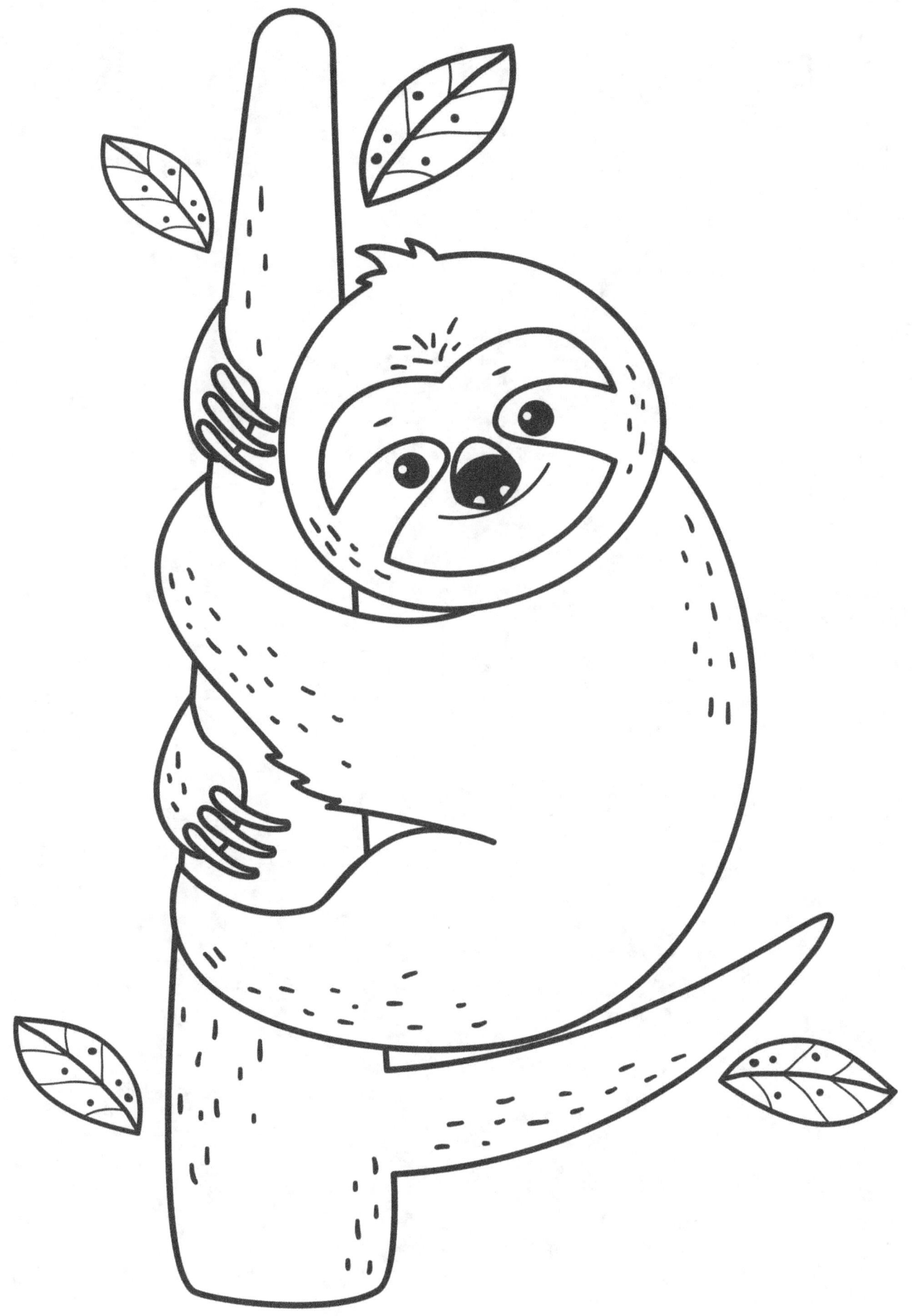

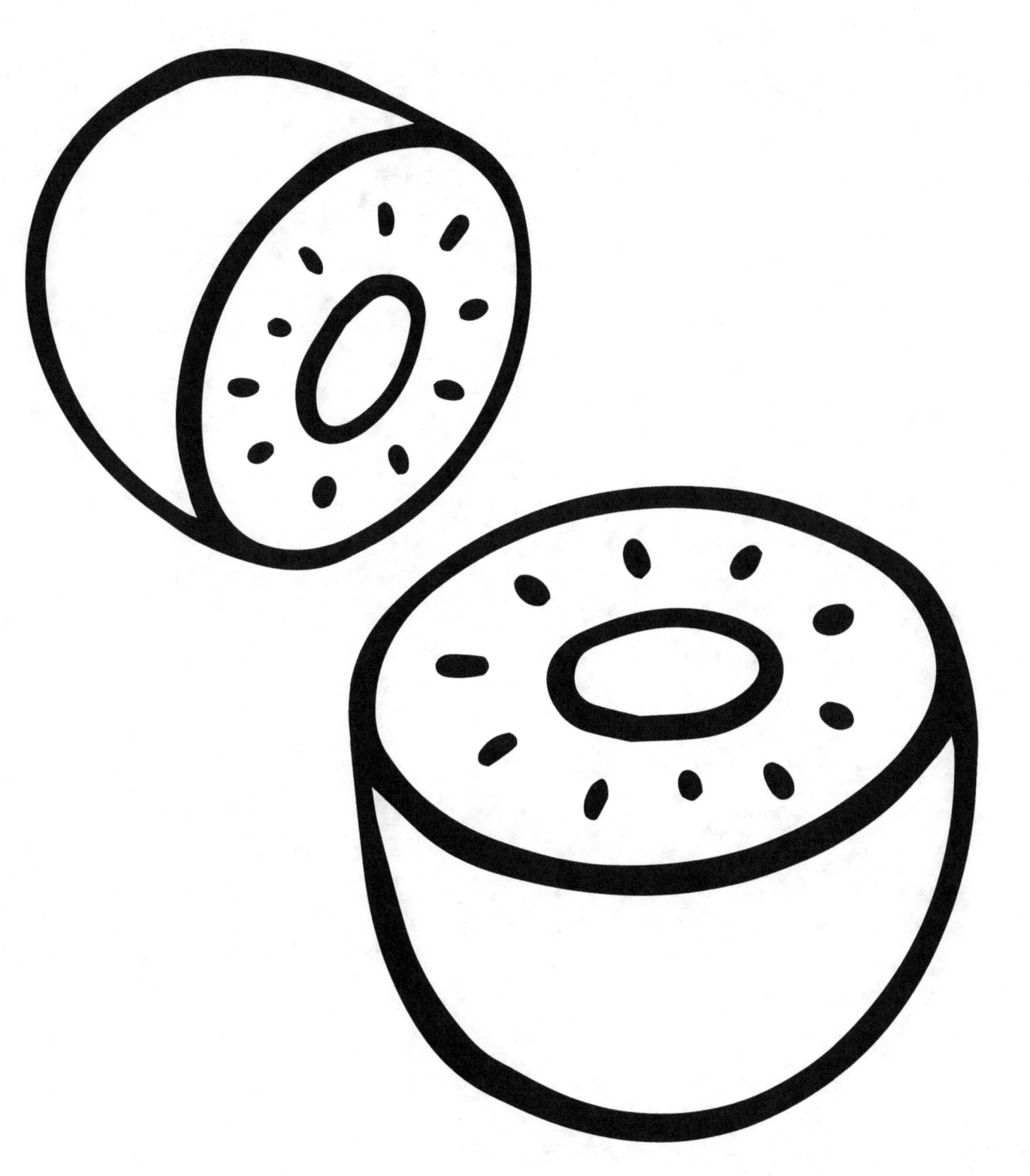

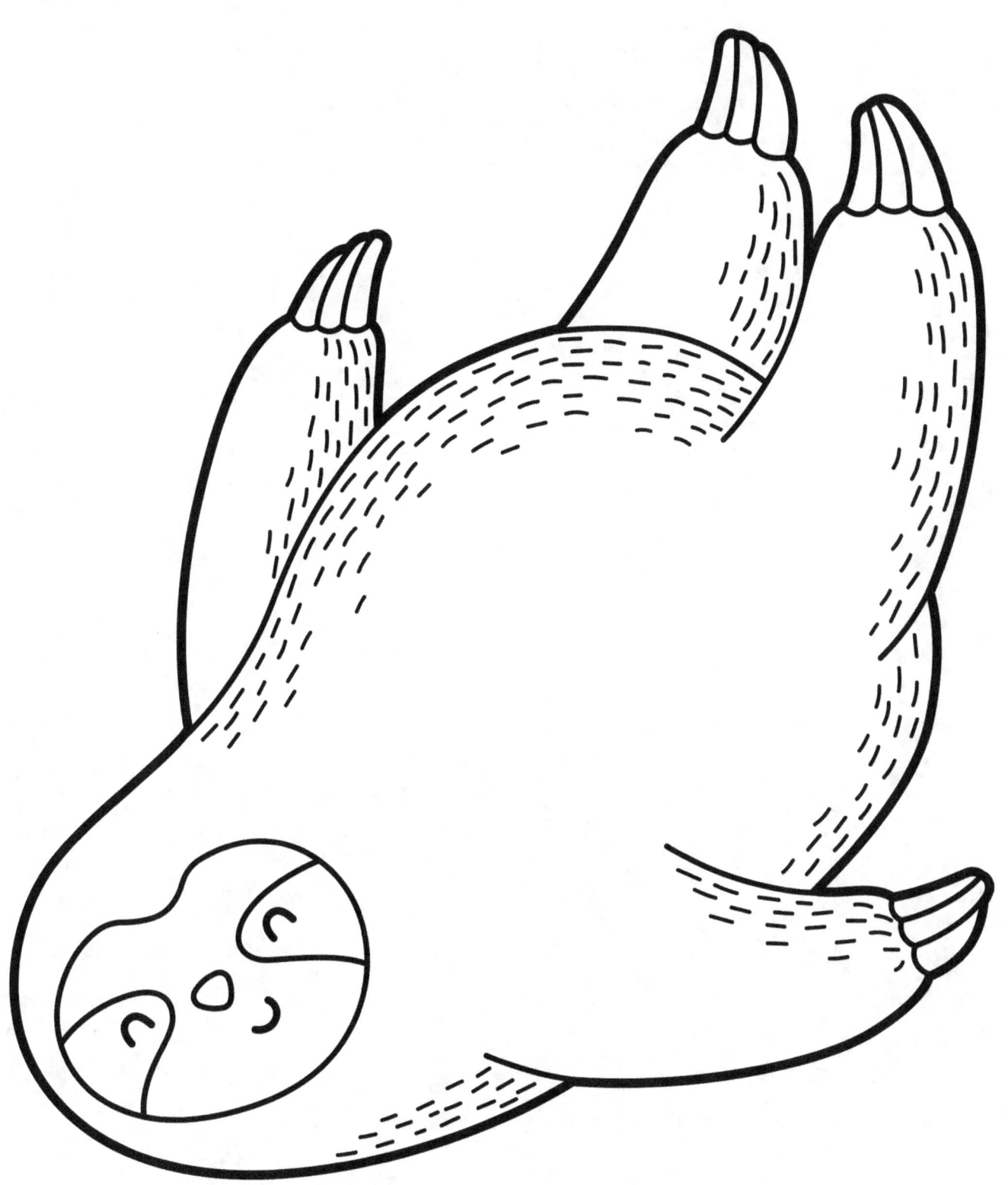

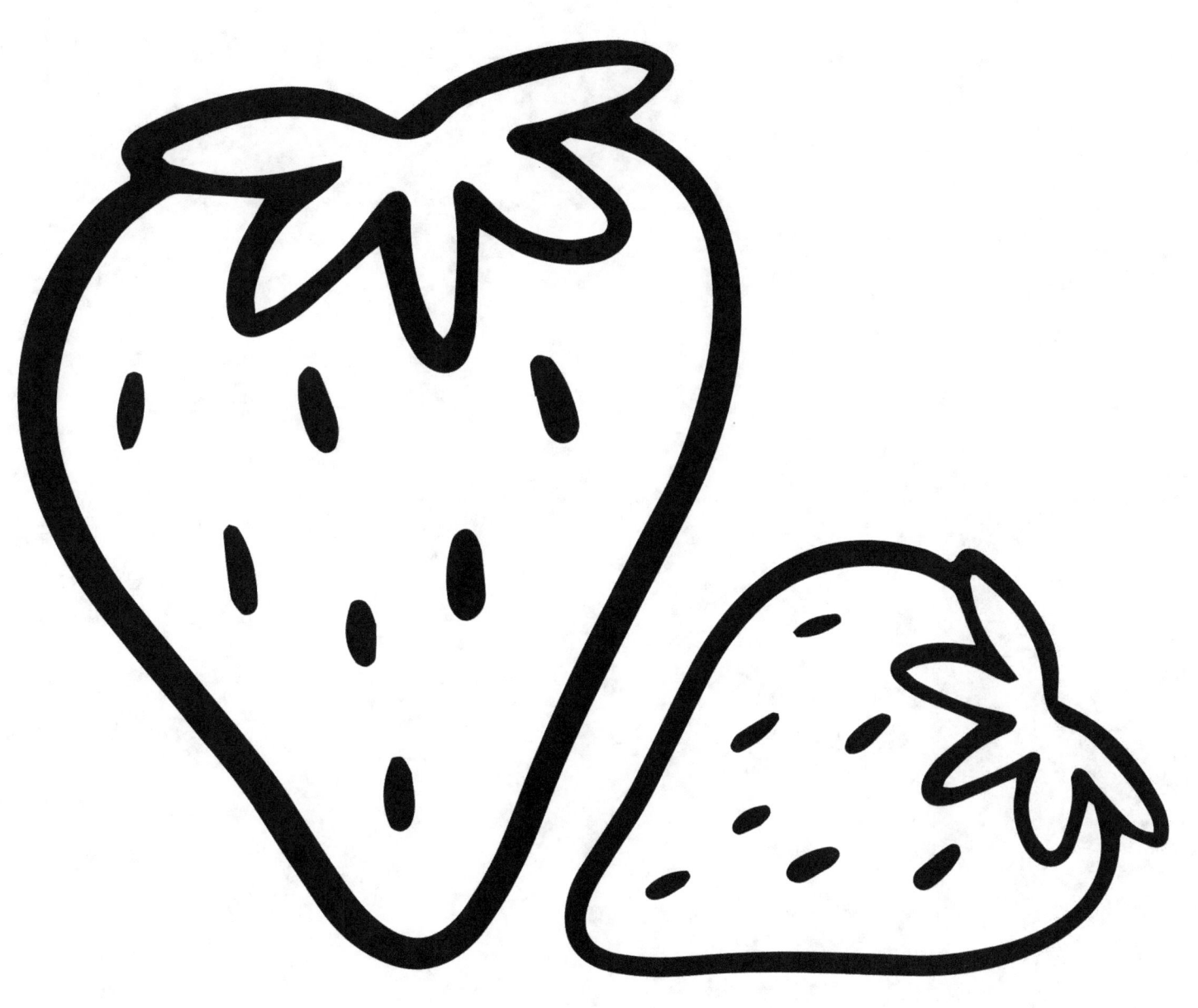

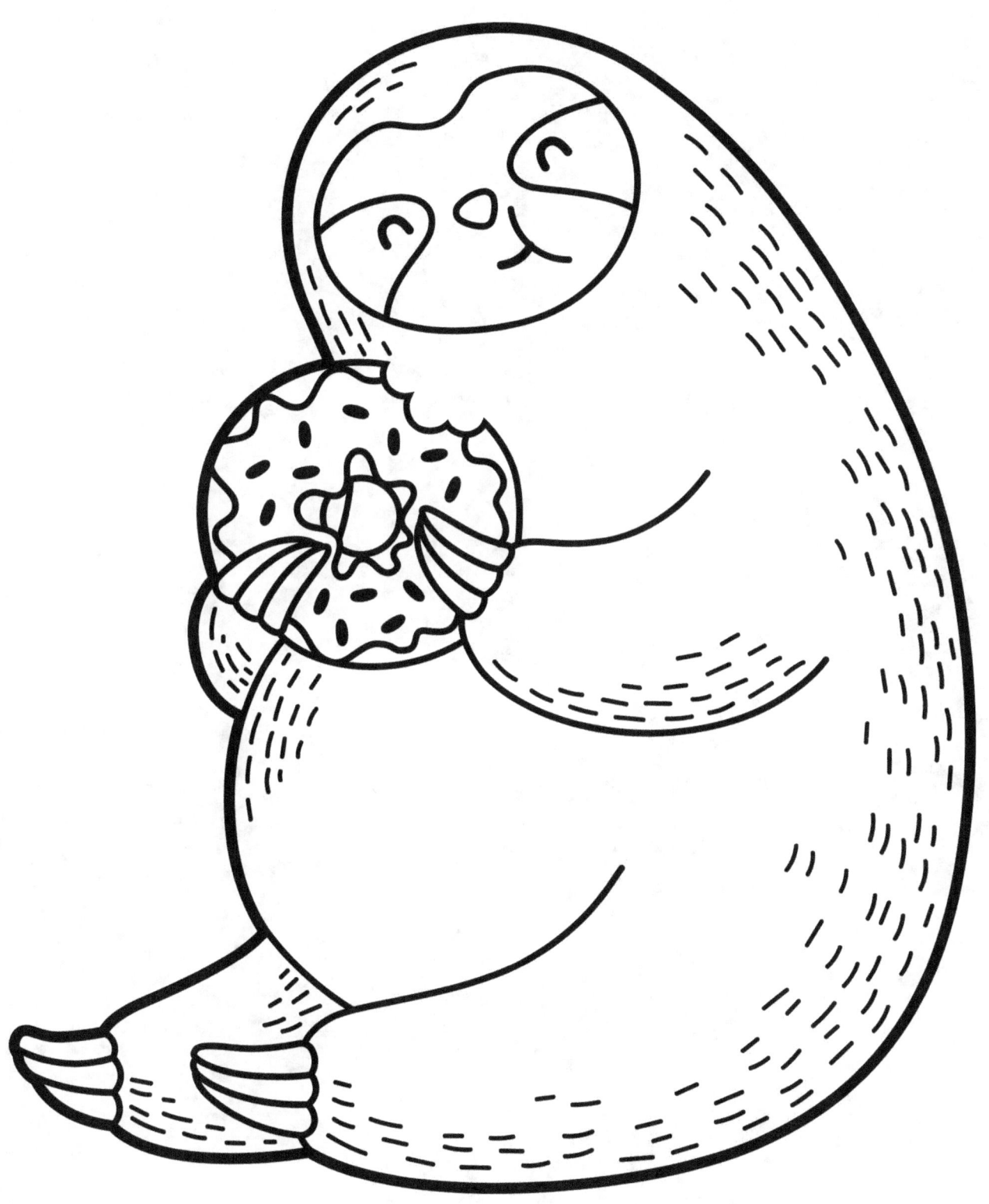

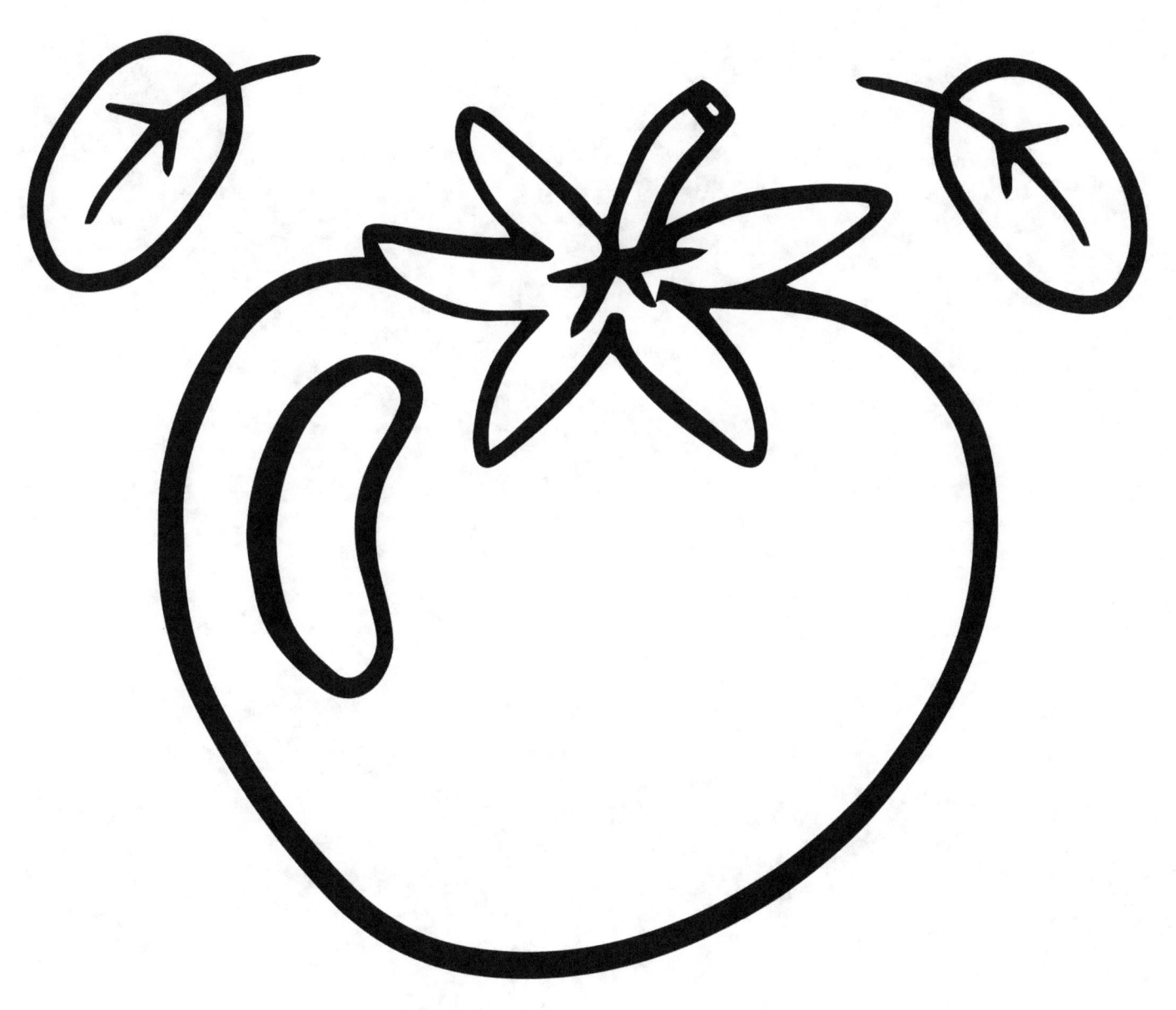

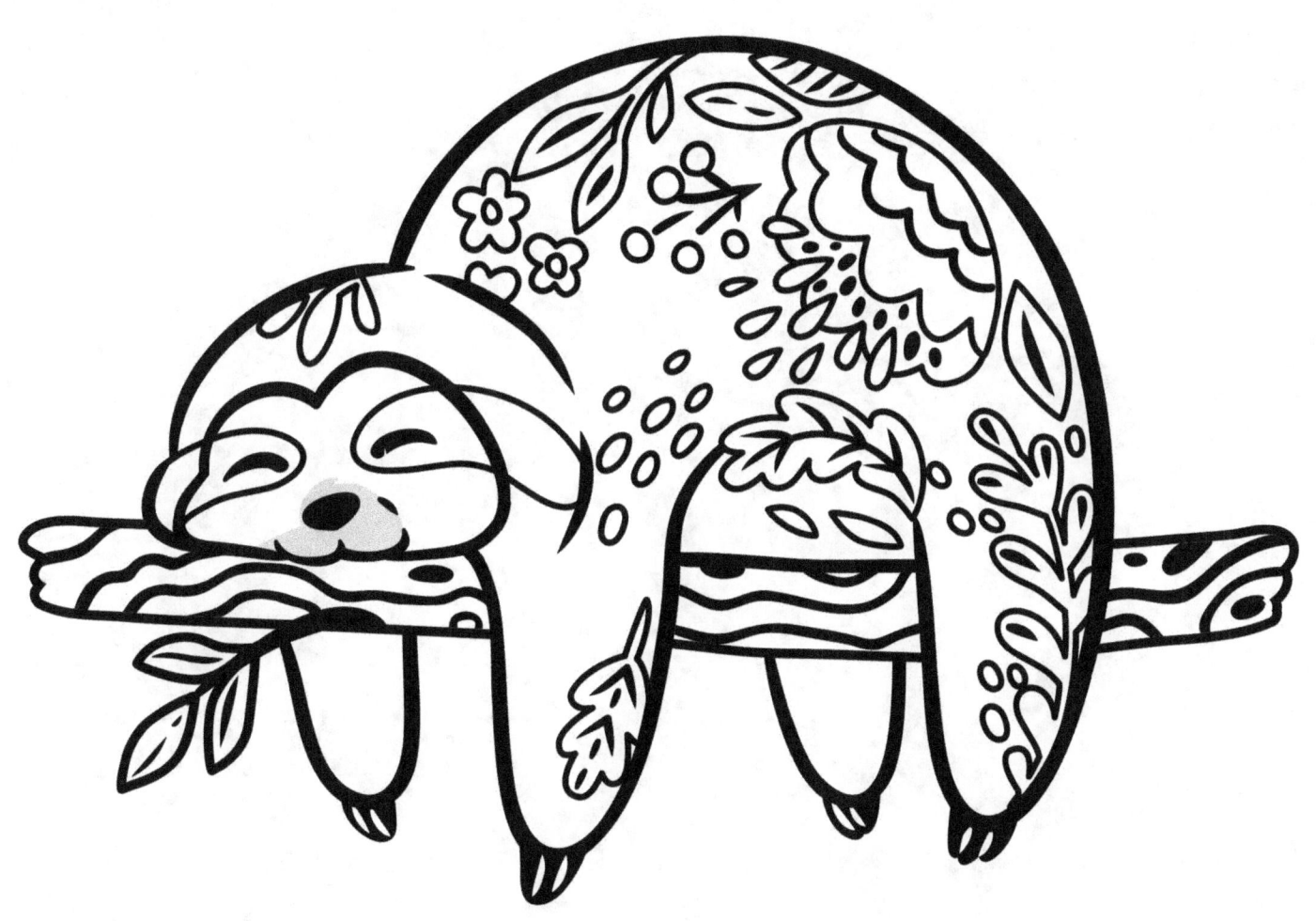

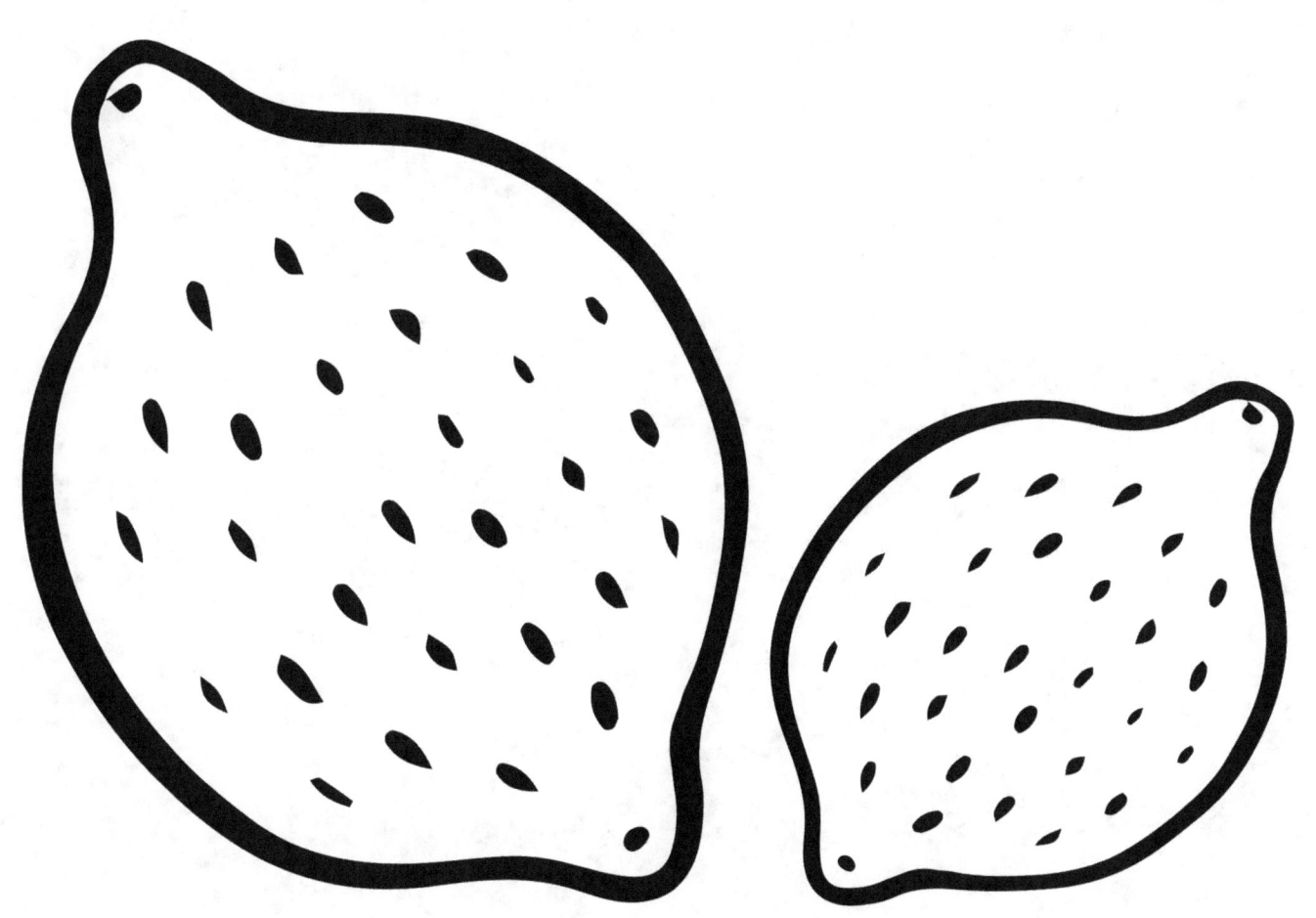

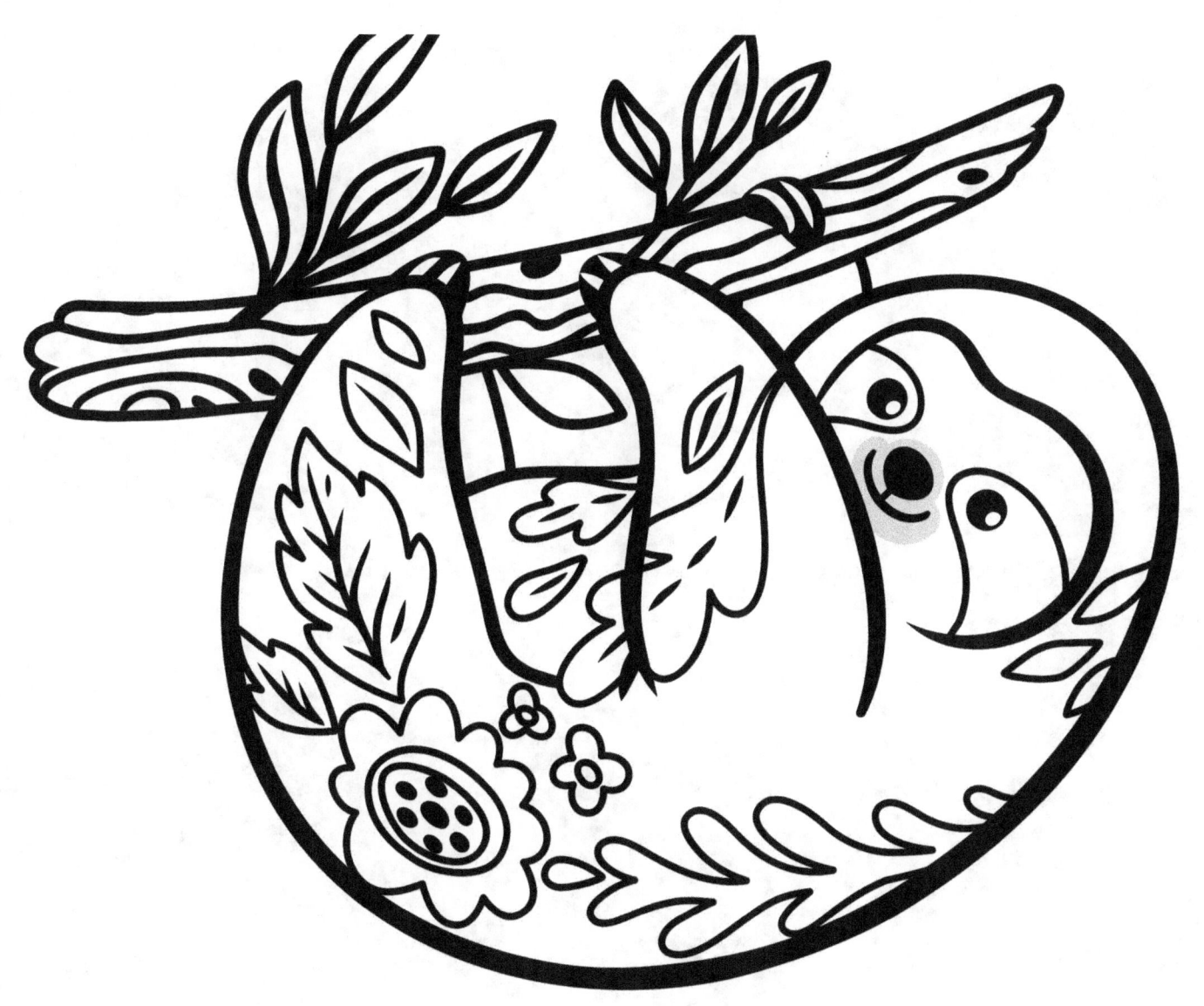

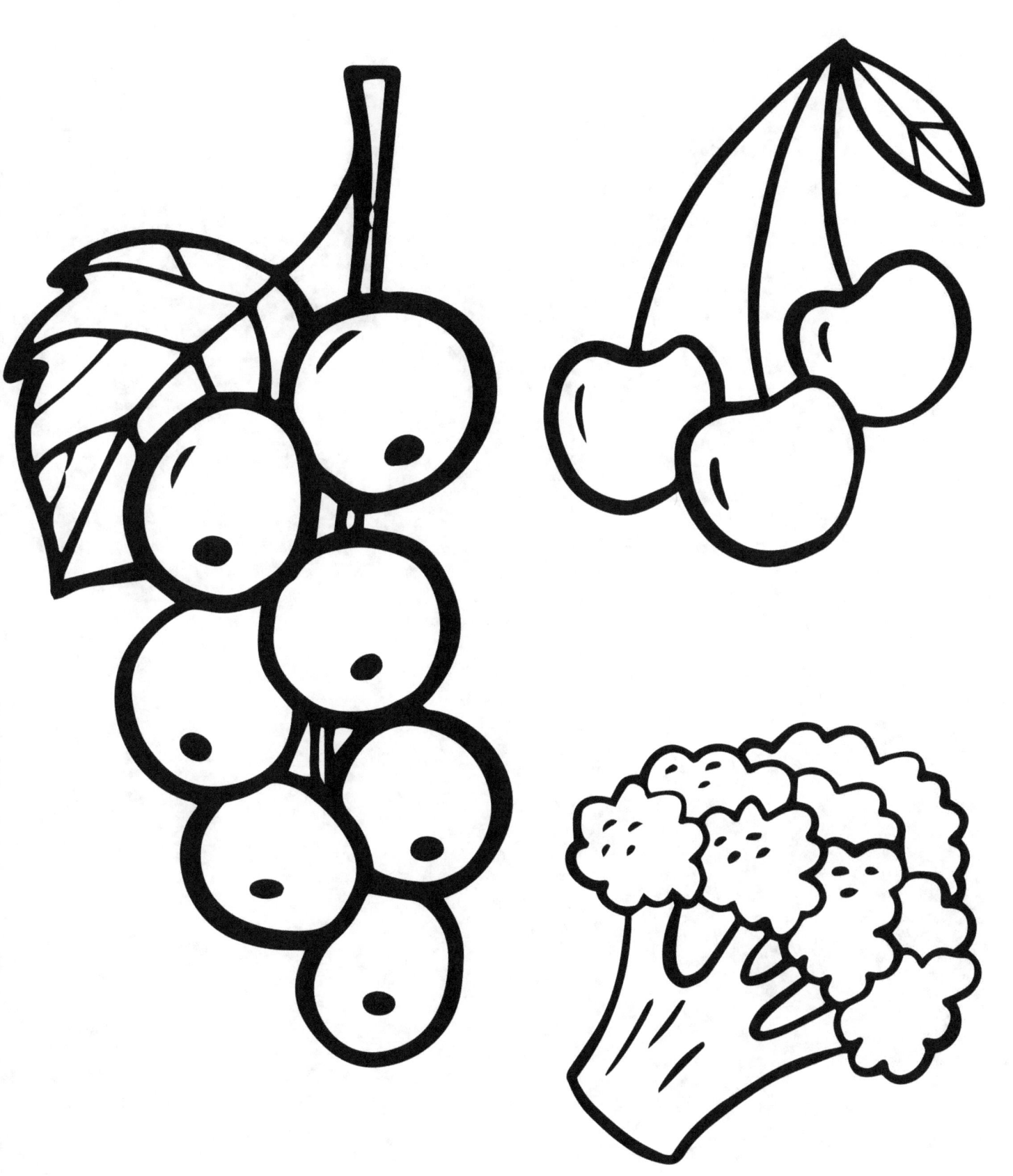

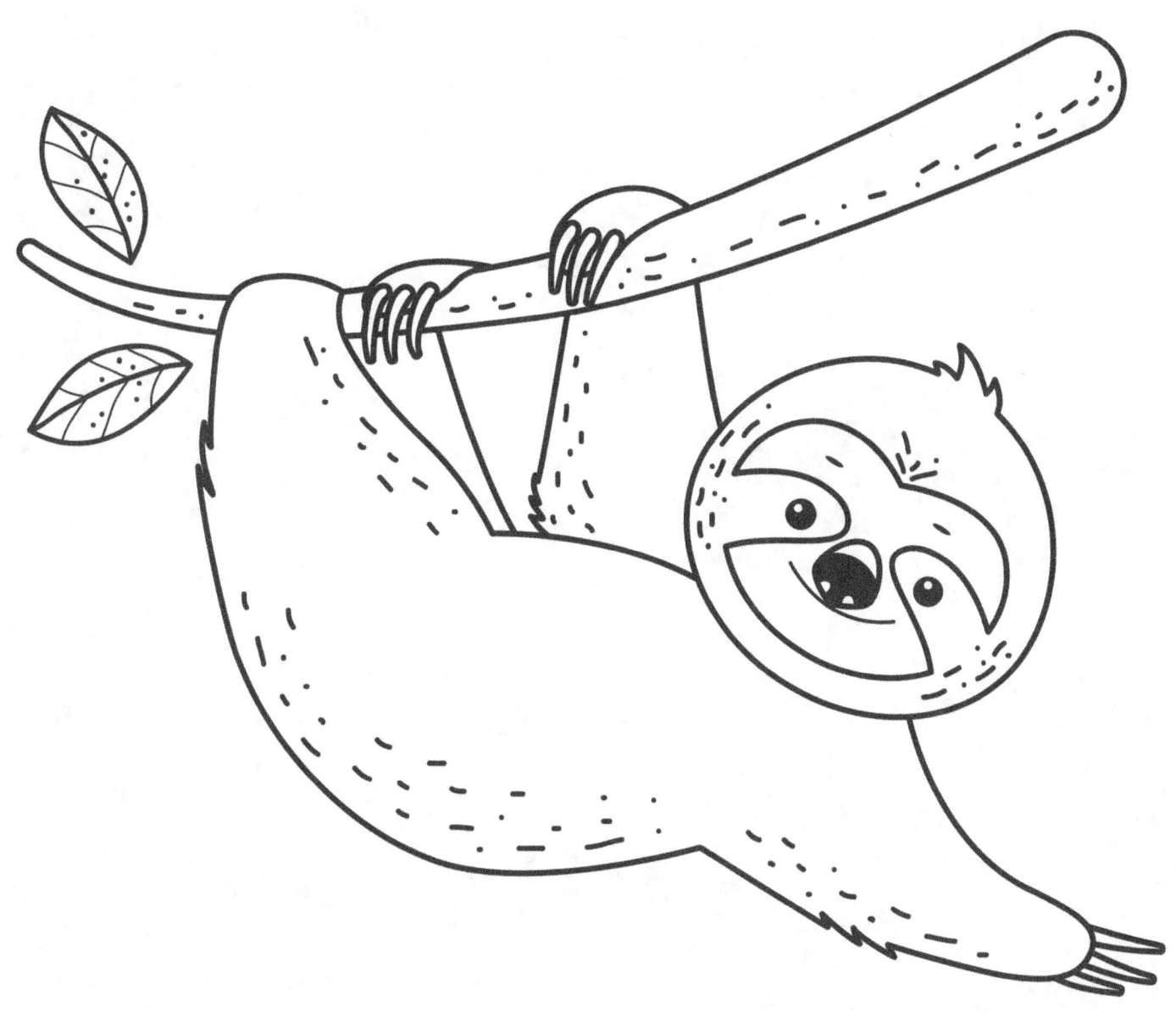

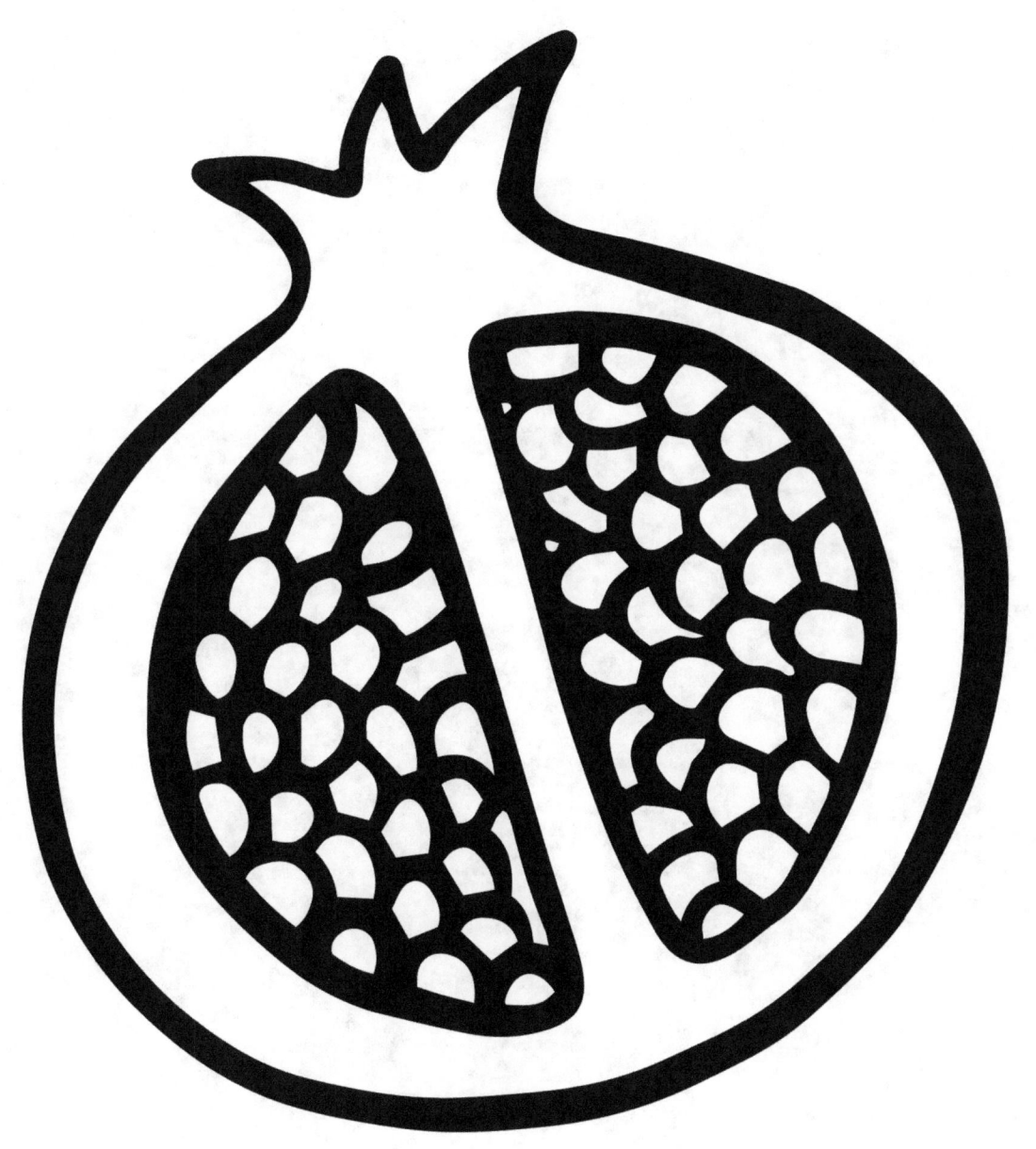

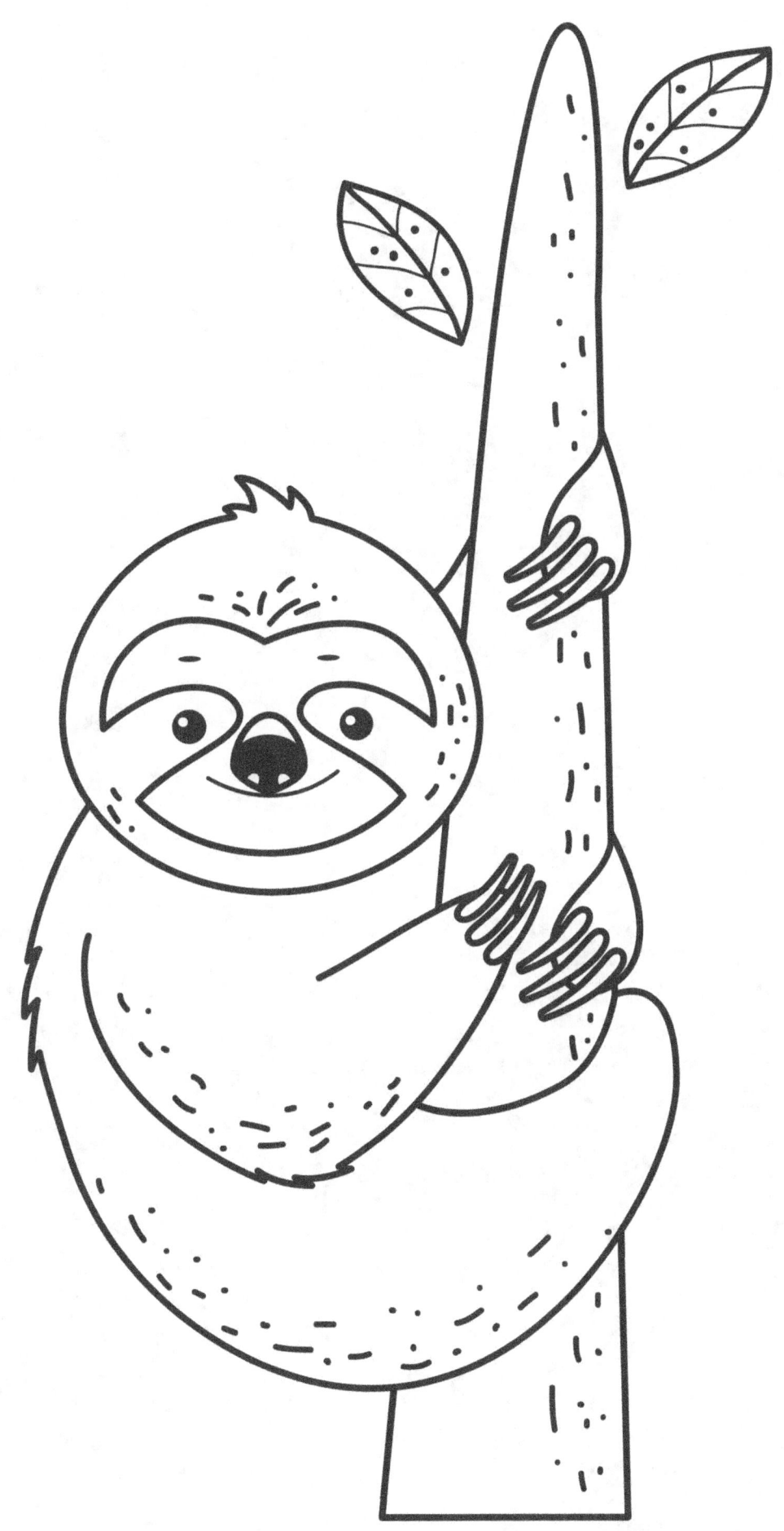

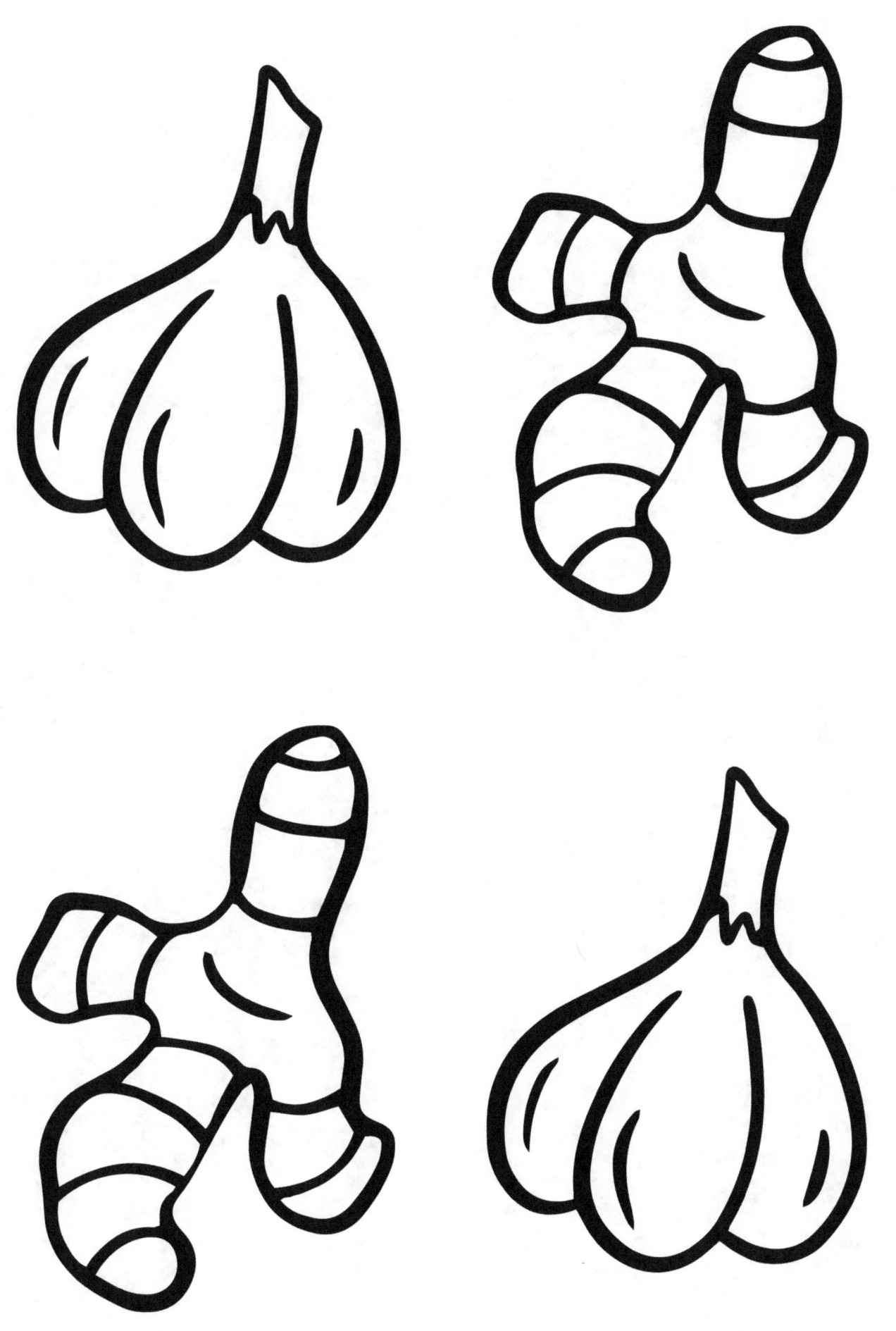

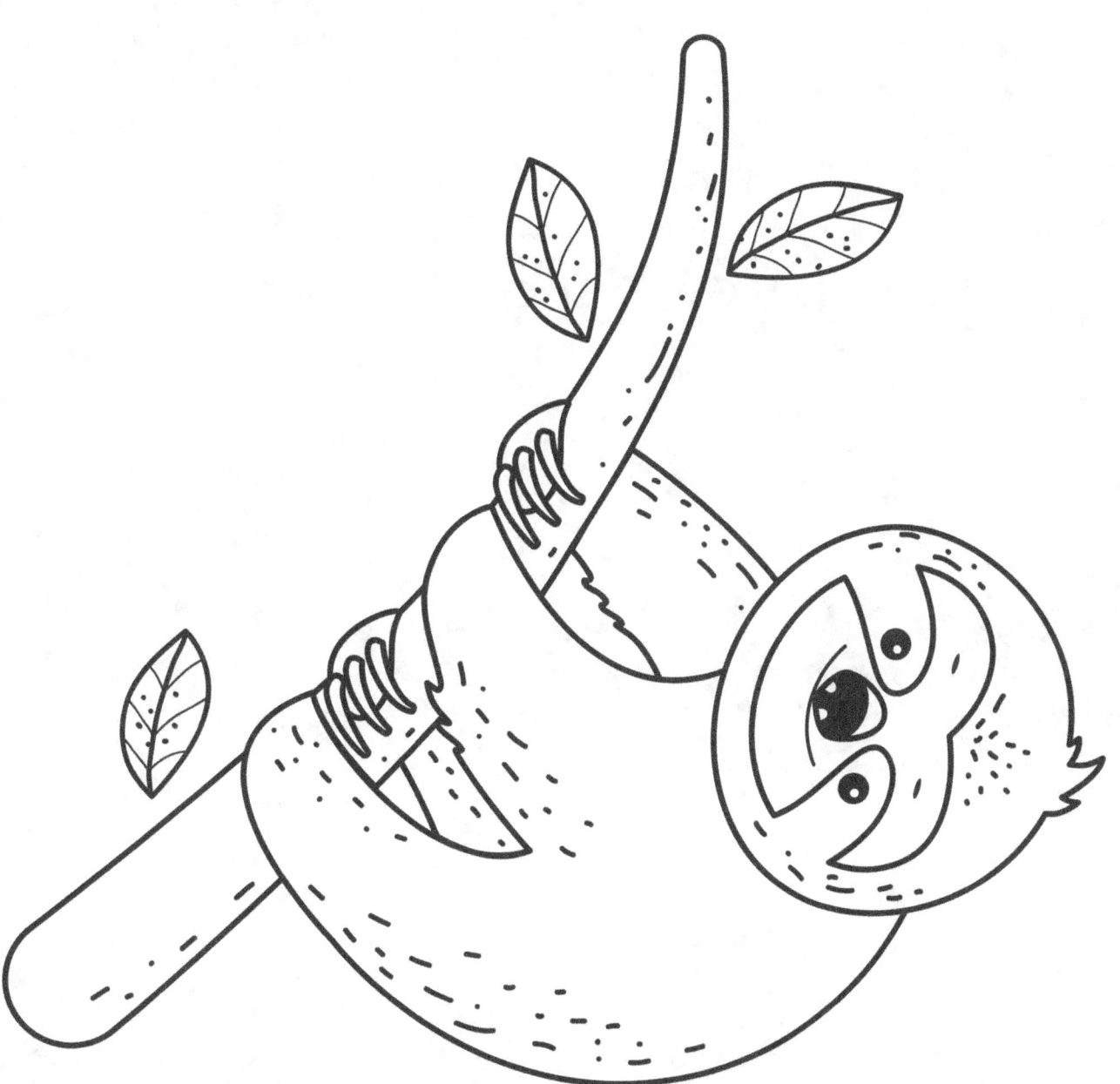

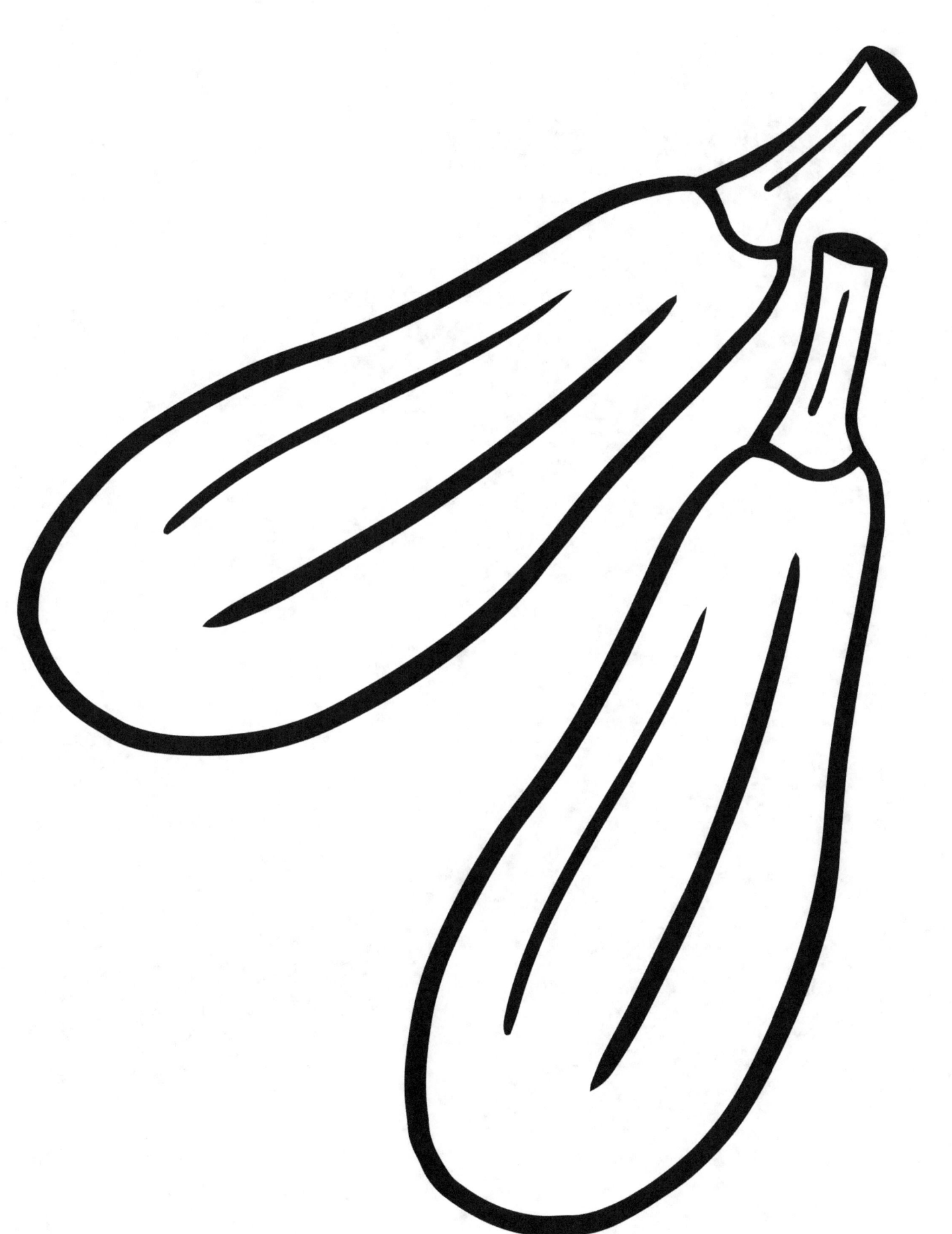

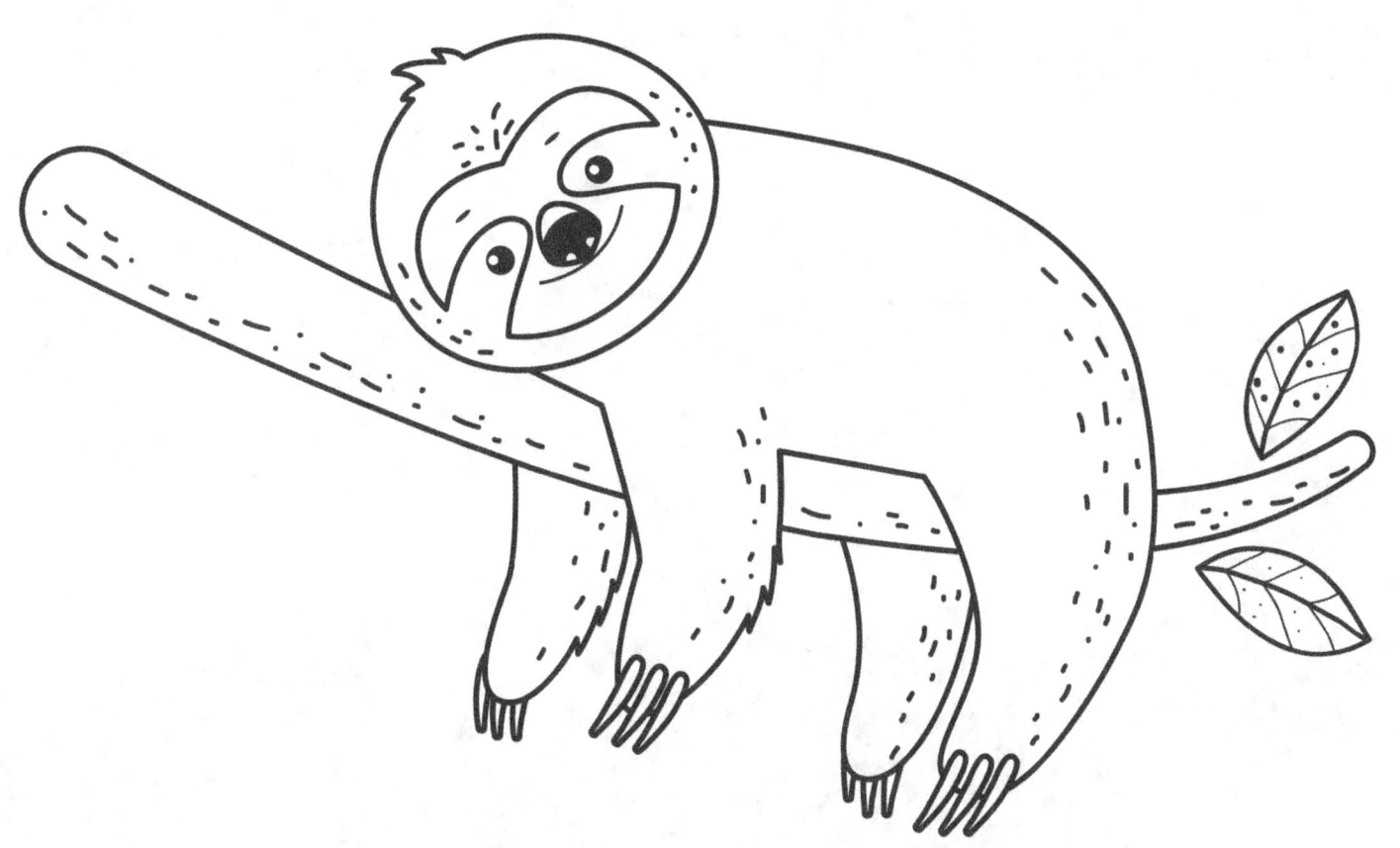

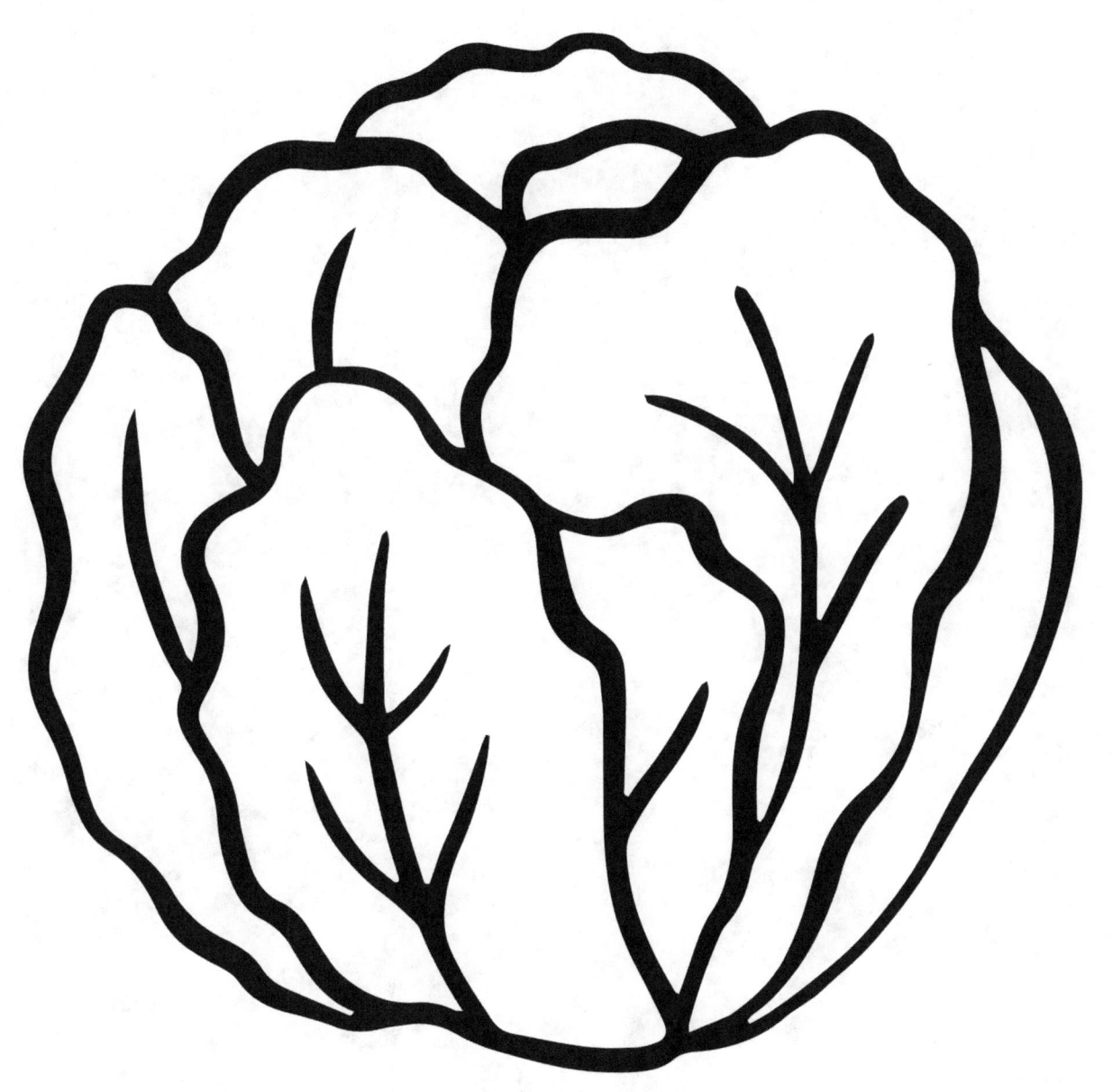

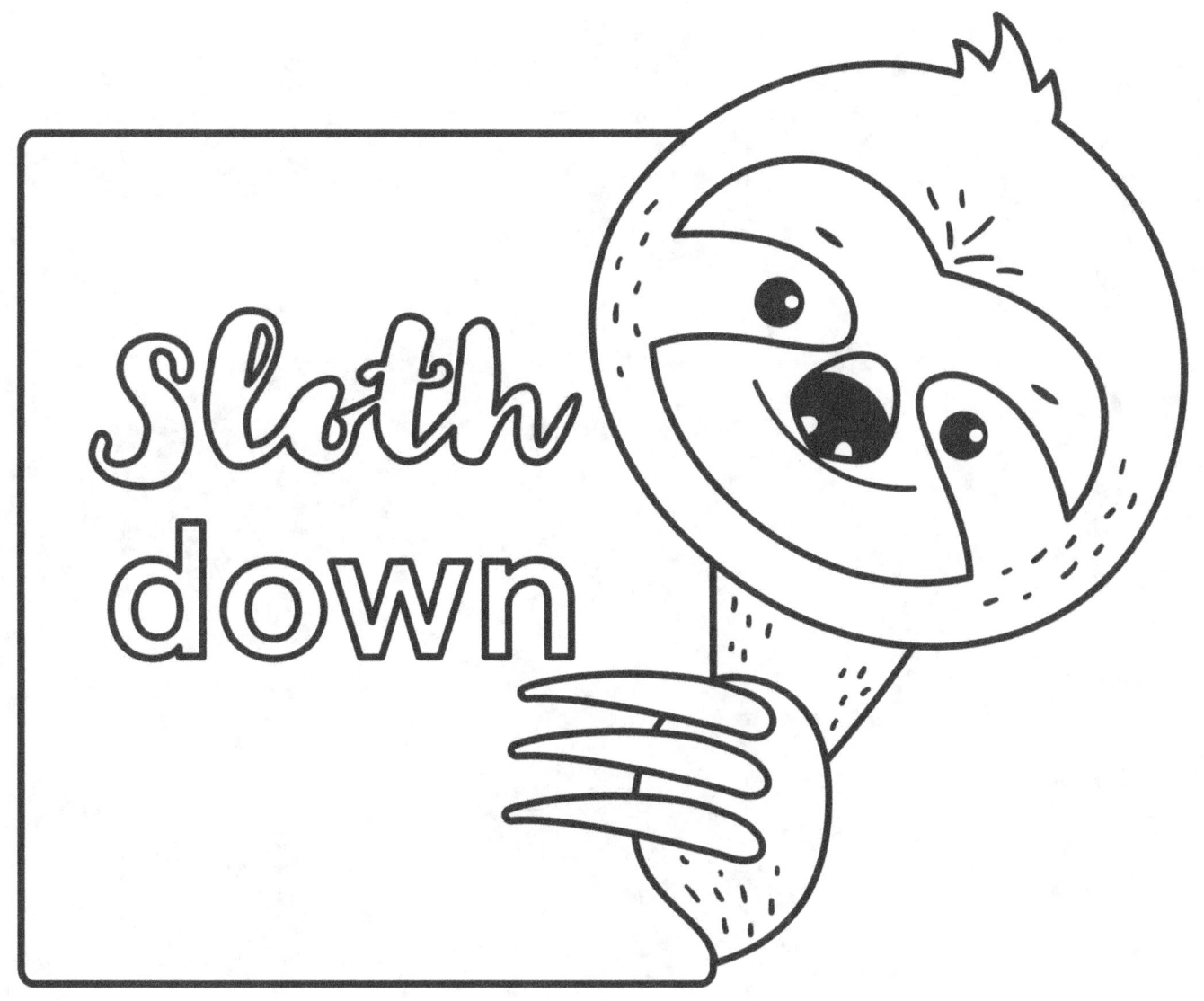

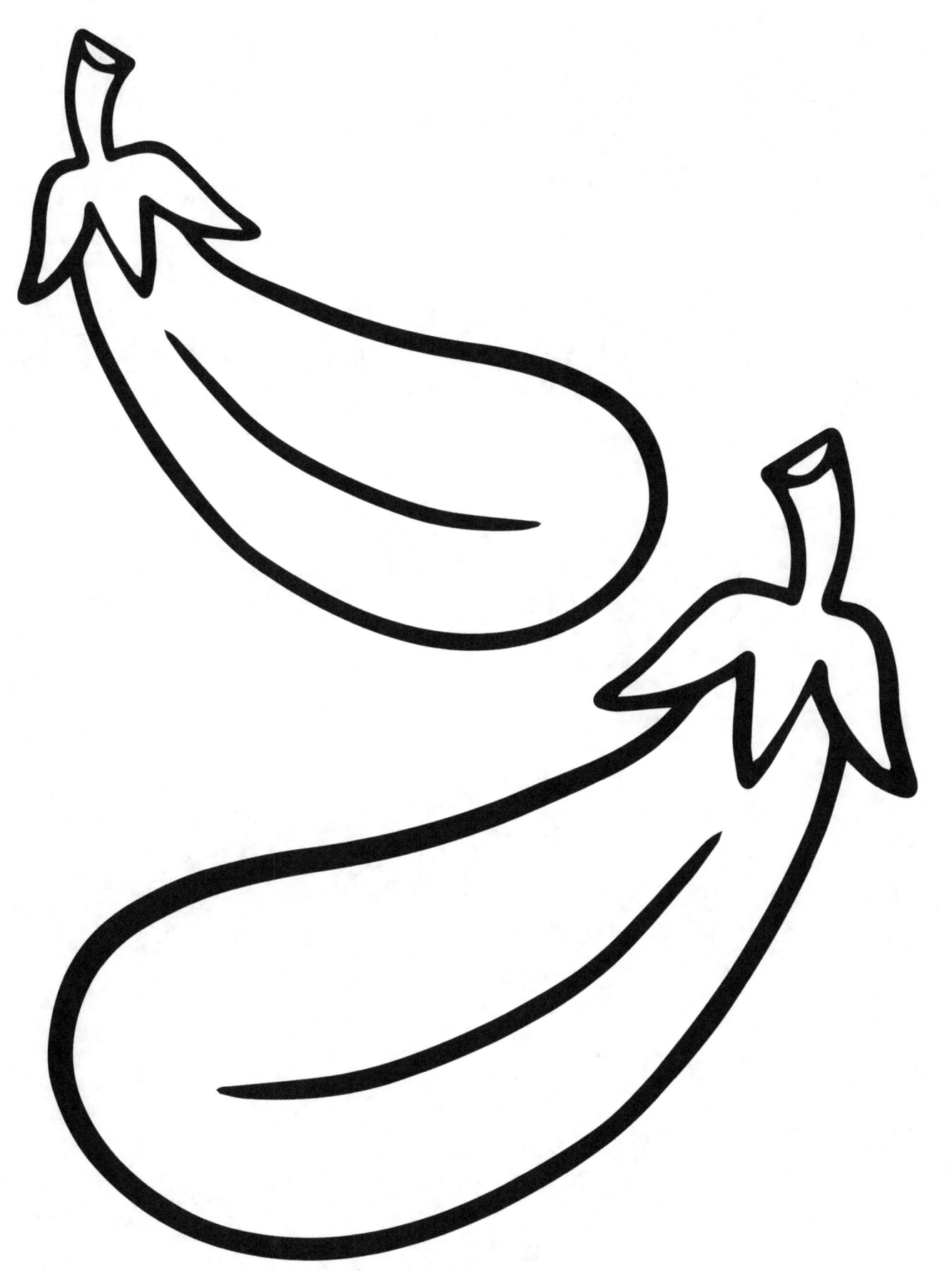

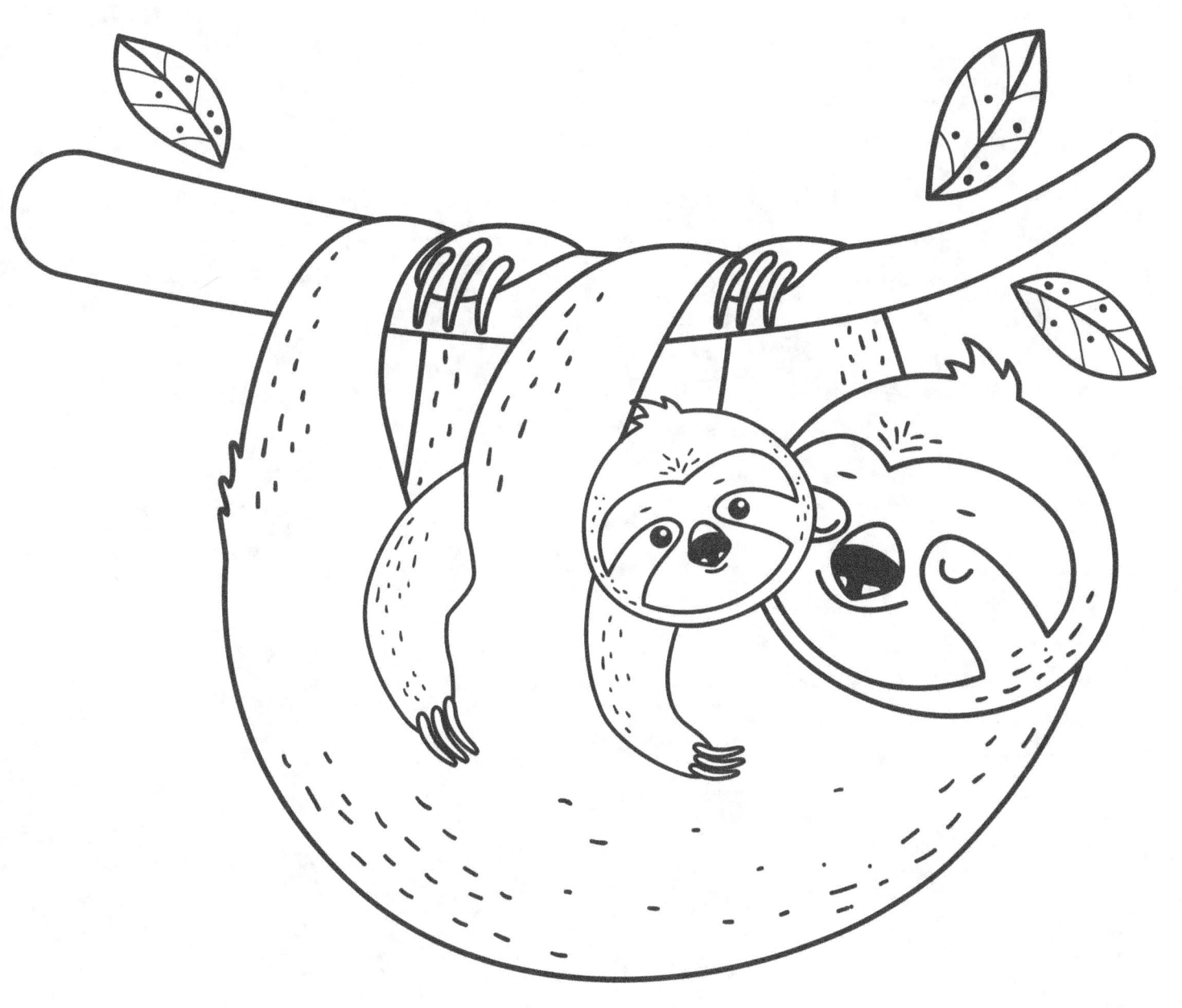

www.ingramcontent.com/pod-product-compliance
Lightning Source LLC
Chambersburg PA
CBHW081449220526
45466CB00008B/2570